FOREWORD

The continent of Europe is in desperate need of pioneers who plant new churches. The contributing authors of M4 have a desire to mobilize people to do church planting in Norway, Scandinavia and Europe. M4 is not formed in an academic environment but out of practical experience. We are church planters ourselves, and we share with you from our own lives and experiences. We come from various church backgrounds and organizations, but we hold certain things in common:

» A passion to see people won for Jesus Christ and new churches planted in Norway, Scandinavia, and Europe.

» A faith to see God raise up thousands of his people, both young and old, with a call and equipping to form and multiply new, vibrant fellowships.

» A longing to be spiritual fathers and mothers for a young generation that needs to hear, "GOD IS ABLE! Just do it! We're standing with you! We believe in you!"

» A belief that "together with all the saints" we can recognize and understand what God is doing today. We desire to listen and learn from each other, in mutual respect and appreciation for the various models and methods used by each other in church planting.

» A conviction that nothing is impossible with God. When we obey and follow the Word of God, he stands by his promises.

M4 has been developed in the church-planting environment of Norway. The National Church Planting Network of Norway is a support network consisting of people who recognize that when we work together as the body of Christ, we will see living churches established in all ethnic, cultural and geographic areas of a nation.

The contributing authors of this book are, in one way or another, involved with the National Church Planting Network of Norway. We've collectively read hundreds of books about church planting, leadership, and pioneer work. We believe that knowledge is a good thing, but action based on what we've learned is even better. Faith grows only through obedience.

For the international version of M4 Part 2 we have the privilege of welcoming Dietrich Schindler as one of our contributing authors. Dietrich writes about the Jesus movement in Europe and draws from his experience and knowledge gained from planting five churches and from leading the church planting efforts of the Evangelical Free Church in Germany.

M4 is developed as a *process tool* and we want to encourage you to be accountable to take action. With a clear foundation in the Word of God combined with the personal experience of the authors, M4 will help you reflect and act on central issues that are relevant for all church planters. If you have a dream to start something new, M4 is a tool to help you to realize your dream.

We are thankful for the pioneers that have gone before us and have shown us the way. They have guided and inspired us to follow the call of God on our lives, which is to establish churches that reach out and save people for the kingdom of God. We feel privileged and thankful to be part of the ever-expanding kingdom of God.

THE AUTHORS

ØIVIND AUGLAND is married to Linda, and they have four children. Øivind is a former church planter and has been a pastor in the Evangelical Lutheran Free Church of Norway for 18 years. He has also been working for the National Church Planting Network of Norway, in recent years as its network planner and manager. Øivind works with issues concerning leadership development, strategy, and organizational development. He also founded the companies Xpand Norway and Persolog Norway.

TERJE DAHLE is married to Lise; they have three adult children and one grandchild. After graduating from nursing school in 1984, Terje moved to Stokmarknes, Vesterålen in northern Norway, and became the leader of Christian Fellowship (Kristent Fellesskap). He also worked as a nurse at the local hospital and completed a degree in leadership at Bodø College. From 1994 to 2001 he functioned in various managerial positions for Telenor until he was offered a full-time position at Christian Fellowship, focusing primarily on pioneer work. In 2005 the family moved to Trondheim where Terje joined Christian Fellowship's church-planting work. Today Terje is the leader of Christian Fellowship's work in Norway and has supervisory responsibility for over 20 churches. He has a broad influence in the kingdom of God through his advisory work in Natural Church Development (Naturlig Menighetsutvikling) and through his position on the board of the National Church Planting Network of Norway.

HARALD GIESEBRECHT is married to Kjersti and they have two sons. Harald is a church planter for the Adventist Church of Norway. He is now the leader of Cornelius Church in Oslo, which he also planted. He is currently creating material for leadership training and discipling. In addition to his work, family and commitment to the National Church Planting Network of Norway, he is working on a Master Degree in theology.

ØYSTEIN GJERME is married to Gina and they have three children. After four years as youth pastor in The Tabernacle Pentecostal Church, he established the Salt Bergen Church where he functions as the main pastor. Øystein holds a Master of Divinity from Regent University and a B.A. in Pastoral Studies from North Central University in the USA. He is the Chair of the College of Leadership and Theology in Oslo where he also teaches homiletics.

ARNT JAKOB HOLVIK is one of the founders of Os Fellowship, a young interdenominational missionary movement that is committed to evangelism, church planting, and missions in the village of Os, located south of Bergen in western Norway. The movement equips church planting teams from different denominations in Norway and Northern Europe. Arnt Jakob is educated in international social science and social economics, and is about to finish a Masters in Theology. He became a pioneer and missionary after Jesus touched his life and sent him out into full-time service. Arnt Jakob now lives and works in a faith-based Christian community in Os in which they share their finances and rhythm of life consisting of prayer and missionary work.

HÅVARD KJØLLESDAL lives in Trondheim and is married to Katrine. Together they have three children. He is a secondary school teacher and has a degree in social science. He is a church planter for Christian Fellowship in Trondheim and works with the online FOLK Bible School.

ANDREAS NORDLI is the leader of Youth with a Mission - Norway, a branch of the international, interdenominational missionary organization Youth with a Mission (YWAM). He is married to Åsne, and they have five children. They live at YWAM-Norway's main missions base at Grimerud, just outside the city of Hamar. He worked for many years in Romania with church planting, leadership training and sending Romanian missionaries to foreign countries. His heart's desire is to send Norwegians out in missions, both to Europe as well as to the unreached peoples of the world.

DIETRICH SCHINDLER (D.Min Fuller Theological Seminary) has been doing church planting in Germany for 28 years. Along with his wife Jan, Dietrich has planted five churches within the German Evangelical Free Church and became the denomination's executive director for church planting in 2008. He is working with others to see a hundred new churches planted in Germany in the next ten years. Dietrich was born in 1958 in Milwaukee, Wisconsin to German immigrants. He is the author of *The Jesus Model: Planting Churches the Jesus Way* (UK: Piquant Ed. 2013).

ARNE G. SKAGEN is married to Kjersti and they have four daughters. Arne is an internationally recognized evangelist who has worked with the organizations Christian Network and Ministries Without Borders for the past 16 years. He teaches and coaches churches in many countries, and he has a natural talent to equip believers to live and function in the power of the Spirit and to bring people to Jesus.

M4 – Part 1

New people – new fellowships

From dream to reality

2nd Edition

Editors:

Øivind Augland

Harald Giesebrecht

Contributing authors:

Øivind Augland

Terje Dahle

Harald Giesebrecht

Øystein Gjerme

Arnt Jakob Holvik

Håvard Kjøllesdal

Andreas Nordli

Dietrich Schindler

Arne Skagen

© 2013 DAWN Norway

Epleveien 26

4635 Kristiansand S

NORWAY

Telephone: (+47) 950 42 260

Email: post@dawnnorge.no

www.dawnnorge.no

www.m4europe.com

Cover and design: Asketic

www.asketic.lv

Layout: Martin Morfjord

www.morfjord.com | Twitter: @morfjord

English translation: Thomas Freitag & Sara Anfindsen

thomas.freitag@gmail.com & SaraAnfindsen@gmail.com

Printed at Amazon

ISBN 97-882-932-5908-4

Table of Contents

HOW TO USE M4

MASTER • MISSION • MULTIPLICATION • MOVEMENT

M4 a resource tool for everyone interested in church planting. But M4 is more than just a resource: it is a *process tool* that helps you explore important issues that may be present from the moment you start nurturing a dream of a new fellowship until the dream has come true. In the end, your dream might become a living community of 30 or more people.

M4 is built on the Great Commission. Our conviction is that all of Christ's followers can be part of creating and multiplying living fellowships of believers. Not everyone can be a pioneer or a church planter, but we can all be part of a working team. The Great Commission applies to us all! For the Great Commission to be fulfilled, we have to see new churches and fellowships planted in Norway, Scandinavia and all over Europe.

Matthew 28:18-20

"All authority in heaven and on earth has been given to me. Therefore go and make disciples of all nations, baptizing them in the name of the Father and of the Son and of the Holy Spirit, and teaching them to obey everything I have commanded you. And surely I am with you always, to the very end of the age."[1]

From the Great Commission we have highlighted *four areas of focus*, each designated with a keyword beginning with the letter M. These areas of focus are:

MASTER: "All authority in heaven and on earth has been given to me."

MISSION: "Therefore go..."

MULTIPLICATION: "...and make disciples of all nations, baptizing them in the name of the Father and of the Son and of the Holy Spirit, and teaching them to obey everything I have commanded you."

MOVEMENT: "   And surely I am with you always, to the very end of the age."

1. "All authority in heaven and on earth has been given to me."

5. Action plan for 1-2 years

2. "Therefore go..."

4. "And surely I am with you always..."

3. "...and make disciples..."

M4 is divided into two books: Part 1 covers M1 MASTER and M2 MISSION, and Part 2 covers M3 MULTIPLICATION and M4 MOVEMENT .

M4 is for everyone who is working to start new fellowships. The books cover essential subjects that everyone involved in church planting can relate to. M4 is intended as a training tool for you and your team. Everything you find in the M4 books is available as video lectures online. You can also find other resource materials online—such as articles and interviews with church planters—which can be useful in your training process.

Two Levels

M4 – two levels

Level 1:

M4 can be used *as a resource for a church planter and for a church planting team*. There are special exercises for you and your team at the end of each M4 section, developed to help you work through the four focal areas we've taken from the Great Commission. The books are designed as a resource tool specifically for the early stages of church planting. When the books are used in a group context, it is important that each team member go through the exercises before moving on to the next section. We recommend that you allocate several meetings with your core team to go through these exercises.

The books contain:

» Four focus areas of the Great Commission – MASTER, MISSION, MULTIPLICATION and MOVEMENT – all of which have secondary themes presented under them.

» Team exercises, case studies, individual exercises and learning goals for each of the focus areas on our website m4europe.com. You will also find on the website a template for a project assignment that can be included as a part of the process. The assignment is based on the work you have done with the other exercises.

Level 2:

M4 can also be used *as a facilitator in bringing church planting leaders and their teams together* – in networking and fellowship, as well as to learn and gain vision from each other's church planting experiences. The authors of M4 are convinced that church planters and their teams need others to help and support them throughout the planting process. Meeting other teams in the same situation can be motivating, encouraging and practical. A meeting like this can be arranged in your region or through the church fellowship, network or organization you are planting through. After several years of working with M4, we see that all teams need to be accountable to others during the planting process to help them keep their focus.

[2] For more information: m4europe.com

Leaders in the Church Planting Network of Norway facilitate a "train the trainer process" for leaders in different nations and denominations who are using M4 as a tool for church planting in their own context. We do this training mainly for leaders who have responsibility for church planting in organizations and churches, and for people who train and coach church planters.[2]

In M4 we invite church planters and their teams to join a process that stretches over a period of 18 months. Together with other church planting teams they will be trained by experienced church planting leaders who coach them through the entire process.

It is possible to organize these seminars on a regional level or specifically for your organization, network or church fellowship. Frequency and length of the meetings can vary based on the individual context. Subjects from M4 are the main focus, but there is also plenty of time to exchange experiences with others, work together with different teams, receive teaching, gather for prayer and intercession, and receive group coaching.

Those who use M4 at Level 2 also receive:

» Access to video lessons and resource material in the interactive online Growdly e-learning platform. All members of the planting teams who join the process will be placed in a classroom with their own web log-in. Individual and team exercises are available there, and it will be possible to connect online with other teams.

» Help, encouragement, and follow-up from trained coaches who offer a high degree of accountability in implementing a goal-oriented church-planting process.

A TOOL FOR THE FIRST PHASE OF CHURCH PLANTING

M4 is only a tool, and the work it takes to benefit from it lies with each and every team. We are convinced that God will build his church through new church plants, and we believe that M4 can provide help for those who participate in this. The process M4 guides you through can help your dream become reality.

You should see your church plant grow to a core group of 30-70 people, who together have developed a clear vision based on clear values, who reach out to people and make disciples, and who live as role models for new members of the fellowship. These people clearly know what God has called their church to, and they have a clear plan on how they will do this in the coming years. These are only a few of the things M4 can help you with.

Church planting, fellowship planting and different models

Throughout the books we use different terms that basically mean the same thing. We talk about the start-up of new fellowships, church planting, community planting, the start-up of missionary and in-between fellowships, planting of faith communities, and much more. Different terms are suited to different contexts, depending on what would be natural for people to say in their own church, network or organization. Regardless of what terms you use, we are sure that M4 will be useful in your context.

Another term currently being used is *replanting*. Replanting describes the process by which a new work is started within the framework of an existing though dying fellowship. We believe that the strategies of M4 would suit the situation of those of you who are working in a replanting ministry as well.

M4 does not present a specific model or method for church planting. We believe, however, that it is important for you to choose a model to work by, in order to help you stay focused on the kind of fellowship you're planting. Which model is best is often dictated by the context a team is working in, while others can choose a model more freely. M4 provides you with questions that help you find the model you're searching for: "Are we planting a local church or a network fellowship? Is a cell-based model[3] or a house church model[4] best for us? If we're planting in a big city, do we look to the great church networks like Hillsong[5] or Redeemer[6] for inspiration? Are we dreaming of a multi-site church[7] or an organic movement?[8] Are we focused on missional fellowships[9] or something even more creative?"[10] We believe that M4 as a process tool can fit into any model, and give you needed help along your journey from dream to reality.

[3] Neighbour, Ralph W. *Where do we go from here? A Guidebook for the Cell Group Church*. Houston, TX: TOUCH Publications, 2000. Beckham, William A. *The second reformation*. Houston, TX: TOUCH Publications, 1997. Comiskey, Joel T. *Home Cell Group Explosion: How Your Small Group Can Grow and Multiply*. Houston, TX: TOUCH Publications, 2002; Comiskey, Joel T. *Planting churches that reproduce; Starting network of simple Churches*. Lima OH: CCS Publishing, 2009.

[4] Simson, Wolfgang: Houses That Change the World: The Return of the House Churches. OM Publishing, 2001. Original Title: Häuser, die Welt verändern. C & P Publishing; Emensbüll, Germany, 1999. Kreider, Larry. *House Church Networks: A Church for a New Generation*. Lititz, PA: House to House Publications, 2001.

[5] www.hillsong.com. See also www.hillsong.co.uk

[6] www.redeemercitytocity.com

[7] Surratt, Geoff, Ligon, Greg and Bird, Varren. *The Multi-Site Church Revolution*. Grand Rapids: Zondervan, 2011.

[8] Cole, Neil. *Organic Church: Growing Faith Where Life Happens*. West Sussex: John Wiley & Sons, 2005. See also the website: www.simplechurch.eu

[9] Breen, Mike and Hopkins, Bob. *Cluster - Creative Mid-Sized Missional*. Sheffield: ACPI ,2009; Stetzer, Ed. *Planting Missional Churches*, Nashville, TN: Broadman & Holman Publishers, 2006; Hirsch, Allan. *The forgotten Ways*. Grand Rapids: Brazos Press, 2006.

[10] Halter Hugh and Smay, Matt. *DNA - The Gathered and Scattered Church*. Grand Rapids: Zondervan, 2010.

Introduction
– by Øivind Augland

"You are never too old
to set another goal or
dream a new dream."
C. S. LEWIS

"When God is at work,
a church is planted. It
is always a miracle."
ED STETZER

Dare to dream

Do you have a dream to start up a new fellowship or church? Do you have a cream to reach new people with the gospel, leading them to Christ and disciple them in a living community of believers? Has God spoken to you about reaching a specific group of people, a neighborhood or a cultural or ethnic group in Norway, Scandinavia or Europe? If the answer is yes, M4 is for you. The Church Planting Network of Norway has worked twenty years with church planting and the multiplication of fellowships. We've seen around 350 new fellowships planted in Norway during the past 15 years. We're also seeing that most denominations, organizations and networks are increasing their focus on starting new fellowships, and planting churches among immigrants is on the rise.

From an historical perspective we see a clear relationship between growth in churches/organizations and their planting of new fellowships. Those that planted new fellowships and churches from the 1960s to today have experienced growth, while those that didn't have stagnated, decreased in membership and in numbers of congregations. The planting of new churches in Norway has *almost* made up for the regression seen in the church in Norway. So we believe that there is plenty of room for new fellowships all over Norway, Scandinavia and Europe - in cities, suburbs, towns and villages.

We also notice that church plants are generally of the same shape and type as the churches that planted them. More people come to faith in the newly planted churches than in older and established churches, and many are doing church services in more creative ways. The reason we see this phenomenon may be that the new fellowships have prioritized relationships above programs. Yet most new churches still choose to have their services on a particular day of the week at a specific location.[11] This is seen both in the Church of Norway and in other denominations. If we take a closer look at England and the church planting movement that was happening there in the 1980s and 1990s, we might be able to better reflect on what's been happening with church planting in Europe as a whole. In "Hope from the Margins" Stuart Murray and Anne Wilkinson-Heys gives us the following description of the church-planting situation in England:[12]

»   Most churches that planted a new church in the '80s or '90s did it only once. Very few of the new churches grew fast enough to be able to plant a new church themselves.

»   The large focus on the need for human or material resources in church planting restricted many smaller churches from planting a new church.

»   A good number of the church plants failed, stagnated or attracted only people who were already saved.

»   Church planting efforts occurred mainly in those areas where there were already a number of churches in the area, while many of the most urbanized areas remained unreached.

There are many good church plants in Norway and we've seen examples where new churches reproduced other new churches. But what's happened in England pretty much describes what we've seen in Norway the last 30 years. Does Murray and Wilkinson-Heys conclude that there isn't a need to do church planting any more? Quite the opposite: "Multiplication of churches will be the most important thing we can do to get on top of the situation in a nation." This is precisely what has happened in England the past ten years with the Anglican Church leading the way with their network "Fresh expressions."[13] When the Archbishop Rowan Williams was to give a definition for *church,* he answered:

> "(Church is) what happens when people encounter the risen Jesus and commit themselves to sustaining and deepening that encounter in their encounter with each other..."

[11] Models from Hillsong, Willow Creek and Saddleback all have a built-in "come to us" structure. I've seen a number of churches succeed with this structure. Those that have succeeded have a clear plan as to how people are taken from visiting a seeker-friendly service toward faith and discipleship

[12] Murray, Stuart and Wilkinson-Heys, Anne. *Hope from the Margins - New Ways of Being Church.* Cambridge, UK: Grove Books, 2000 (pp 4-5).

[13] Williams, Rowan et.al. *Mission-shaped church; church planting and fresh expressions of church in a changing context.* London: Church House Publishing, 2004.

[14] See www.acpi. org.uk

Why such a definition of the church? One of the reasons is found in the ongoing discussion of the concepts of church and church planting. We often receive traditional associations when we hear the expression "church planting"– like 'repeating what we already know'. Through "Fresh Expressions" the Anglican Church seeks to motivate and help people find new ways of planting churches by making room for creativity and diversity. When working with the "Mission-shaped Church" they came to the conclusion that churches *by their very nature* should be focused on mission and become incarnate in the context they are planting in.[14]

We're seeing the same thing happen all over Europe. God is raising up an army of pioneers, both young and old, who are no longer satisfied with the current situation. They're daring to go out, pioneer new works and start up new fellowships. People are getting saved and entering God's Kingdom. They are a new army of God's people walking in the way of Jonathan, son of Saul, king of Israel. We'll take a look at the story of Jonathon now.

WHETHER BY MANY OR BY FEW – WHO CARES!

[15] 1 Samuel 14:6-10

As a means to describe the situation of the church in Europe today, I feel that God keeps reminding me of and speaking through one particular story in the Bible. It is found in the first book of Samuel, Chapter 14:

> Jonathan said to his young armor-bearer, "Come, let's go over to the outpost of those uncircumcised men. Perhaps the Lord will act in our behalf. Nothing can hinder the Lord from saving, whether by many or by few." "Do all that you have in mind," his armor-bearer said. "Go ahead; I am with you heart and soul." Jonathan said, "Come on, then; we will cross over toward them and let them see us. If they say to us, 'Wait there until we come to you,' we will stay where we are and not go up to them. But if they say, 'Come up to us,' we will climb up, because that will be our sign that the LORD has given them into our hands."[15]

The Israelites were under great pressure and those in Saul's army were hiding in caves from the Philistine army. They had pulled back, given up, and were scared about what might happen to them. Suddenly a young man shows up: Jonathan, Saul's son! Jonathan wants to know what God thinks about the situation. Jonathan knows God, and he knows that God does what he says he's going to do—whether through many or few, it doesn't matter. His knowledge of God combined with a desire to know what God wants to do in the situation gives Jonathan the courage to act. He takes with him just one armor-bearer and goes out to face the Philistines. Jonathon did just one thing right when it comes to good war strategy: He didn't go out to face the enemy alone!

Jonathan experiences that God is with him—he is given the victory over the Philistine garrison. But what happens next is even more amazing. Because of Jonathan's faith, the ways of God unfold before the very eyes of all of Saul's army, giving them the courage they need to come out the caves and fight alongside Jonathan. Soon even the Israelites who had defected to the Philistine side joined ranks with Saul's army—to fight against the Philistines!

God doesn't need a lot of people, but he does need someone who dares to believe him and stand on what he says. Great things can be accomplished for

[16] Joel 2:8

[17] Greg, Pete and Blackwell, David. *24-7 Prayer Manual.* Colorado Springs: David C. Cook, 2010

God when this happens. God needs someone who will go in obedience to restore faith, hope and a sense of his empowering presence to a church that has given up and hides in fear for what might happen to them.

I find the story of Jonathan descriptive of what God is doing in Europe today. God is raising up young pioneers and church planters who dare to say: "Let's see what God is going to do! Whether we are many or few— who cares? We know that GOD HAS SPOKEN."

These people are found both within and without traditional churches and fellowships. They conquer new land and do things we haven't seen before. They bring the church to the marketplace and give it new forms. They create a little army together. In the words of Joel, "They do not jostle each other; each marches straight ahead. They plunge through defenses without breaking ranks...."[16] When Pete Greg initiated the 24-7 prayer movement, he had a vision of an army:[17]

> The vision is JESUS – obsessively,
> dangerously, undeniably Jesus.

> The vision is an army of young people. You see bones?
> I see an army. And they are FREE from materialism....
> They are mobile like the wind, they belong to the
> nations....They are free yet they are slaves of the hurting
> and dirty and dying. What is the vision? The vision
> is holiness that hurts the eyes....It scorns the good
> and strains for the best. It is dangerously pure.

> Light flickers from every secret motive, every private
> conversation. It loves people away from their suicide leaps,
> their Satan games. This is an army that will lay down its
> life for the cause. A million times a day its soldiers choose
> to lose that they might one day win the great 'Well done'
> of faithful sons and daughters. Such heroes are as radical
> on Monday morning as Sunday night. They don't need

fame from names. Instead they grin quietly upwards and hear the crowds chanting again and again: "COME ON!"

Whatever it takes they will give: Breaking the rules.... Laying down their rights and their precious little wrongs, laughing at labels....They are incredibly cool, dangerously attractive --- inside....With blood and sweat and many tears, with sleepless nights and fruitless days, they pray as if it all depends on God and live as if it all depends on them.

And this vision will be. It will come to pass; it will come easily; it will come soon. How do I know? Because this is the longing of creation itself, the groaning of the Spirit, the very dream of God. My tomorrow is his today. My distant hope is his 3D. And my feeble, whispered, faithless prayer invokes a thunderous, resounding, bone-shaking great 'Amen!' from countless angels, from [heroes] of the faith, from Christ himself. And he is the original dreamer, the ultimate winner. Guaranteed. (From The Vision)

Don't look back—GO! Just start moving. When you walk in obedience you will restore hope to the church in Europe. It needs once again to *see,* to *experience* and to *recognize* that God is a living reality in our world. He has not given up on Europe. He longs to show his sovereignty to a continent where people have rationalized away the reality of faith. Just start moving. GO! Be like Jonathan. When you are obedient, you join the ranks of those who bring hope, faith and the presence of God to the people around you. There will come a day when the church in Europe will rise again, come out from its hiding place and conquer the land they've been promised. Then the Kingdom of God will once again be seen on our continent. Be one of those who lead the way to make this happen.

[18] Tolfsen, Øyvind. *The Swedish Research* 2011.

[19] Matthew 16:18

[20] Matthew 28:18-20

DO WE NEED NEW CHURCHES?

Are you one of those who say, "Well, of course we need new churches. What a stupid question!" Unfortunately not everyone thinks this way. You might have met others who say "Don't we have enough churches already? We should just work on filling up the ones we have." If we look at Sweden, between the years 2000 and 2010 an average of one church a week shut down.[18] The decline of membership in denominations and organizations has been so dramatic there that, if the trend continues at the same rate, evangelical churches will be 'history' in Sweden in 50 years. The leaders of several churches and organizations recognize this fact and are now intensely focusing on planting new churches and fellowships. Sweden will need one thousand new churches in the next ten years *just to prevent the decline from continuing.*

So do we need to see new churches planted in Europe? The answer is YES! In the next section we present other arguments as to why church planting is so essential.

Church planting is biblical

Jesus says that he will build his church.[19] The Great Commission sends us out to disciple every people and ethnic group.[20] In the book of Acts we read the story about the advancement of the gospel, and how word about God gained such power that the church spread into all areas of society. The only way this could have happened was that new churches were planted and that these in turn multiplied new churches. As seen in nature, multiplication is the only way life can be passed on to the next generation. In a church planting situation, it goes like this: First, we preach the gospel of Jesus Christ. Second, people get saved. Third, new believers gather together in fellowship. Fourth, a new church is formed. If multiplication is true in nature, it is also true in a Christian fellowship. It's that simple.

Church planting is effective

Church history shows us that it is often more effective to start a new, outward-looking church than to try to change the sedentary attitudes of an established church. Change and renewal for established churches is of course important, but it should not get in the way of our focus on planting *new* churches. Established churches often experience difficulty in reaching out to new people. New fellowships, however, have a special vitality and vision that attracts new people and leads them to repentance and surrender to Jesus. Research shows that in Sweden, twenty-five percent of all baptisms take place in new churches. And *new churches only represent eight percent of all churches in Sweden*. This demonstrates that new churches three times more effective at reaching out to new people than established churches. This also indicates that as churches become more established, they become less effective in reaching out to new people.

Church planting is necessary for the life and vitality of a denomination

Statistics from church denominations in Europe show that there is a clear relationship between church planting and growth in different church settings. Church denominations and organizations that do not engage in church planting and start new fellowships go into decline. Church planting is a necessity for life and vitality of a church denomination. God is the God of the generations; He is the God of Abraham, Isaac and Jacob. A family can only continue to the next generation by having children. The history of the European Church shows us that church denominations and organizations that do not multiply by raising up new leaders and new churches die-out within three generations.

Church planting imparts vision

We need to ask ourselves good questions to find good solutions. Some ask: "Why plant new churches when there's still plenty of room in the old ones?" or "Why bother to plant a Pentecostal church in a city that already has one?" These are the wrong questions. If you focus on these kinds of questions you will reach false conclusions. But having a vision spurs us to ask good questions: "Who hasn't been reached with the gospel yet? How can we reach them? What kind of church model can help us reach these people? What's important to them and what are they concerned about? We can't wait for people to come to us – we've got to go to them!" If leaders don't paint alternative pictures for the future, we end up repeating what we're already doing today. A vision for church planting releases pioneers who dare to break new ground.

Church planting breeds new leaders

Church planting is the perfect arena to challenge new leaders in their development. It releases new resources and people with energy, courage, time, talents, finances and vision.

Church planting makes the passive active

The goal of church planting is to reach new people. But in Norway and Europe many people have drifted away from the church and their faith. New churches have the chance to reach these people, to revitalize their faith and to bring them into a committed fellowship where they can grow in their Christian lives.

LESSONS FROM OUR RECENT CHURCH-PLANTING HISTORY

[21] 1 Corinthians 13

During the last thirty years we've noticed that church plants in Norway have been getting healthier. For example, fewer newly planted fellowships close down today than in the '80s. Maybe some of the things we've learned through the years can also help you plant a church in a healthier way. We share some of the things we've learned below.

Not in rebellion or arrogance – but with a servant's heart: The attitudes a church planter has can be decisive for the future of a new church. A church planted with a mind polluted by pride, arrogance and rebellion can only bear bad fruit. Leaders who are angry or rebellious – those who want to plant a new church because they think they can do it better or want to make their mother church look bad—are not ready to plant a new church. We are called to bless and not to curse, to walk in faith and forgiveness – not in accusation.

Relationship and discipleship first: Not programs, not buildings, but people come first. Church planting is about people, not activities. Our goal should always be sharing the gospel with others, lead them to Christ and disciple them to become mature in their lives and ministry. Quality programs are good, but they must be seen as a means and not the end in church planting.

Not alone – but together: You have to prioritize and create good teams to bring out the diversity of spiritual gifts that are required to start a healthy community. A single individual with an extraordinary combination of talents and gifts is not enough. Character goes before charisma. Gifts will cease, but love never fails.[21] This is important to think about when you search for team members. Loving relationships between the members in the core team is a strong and healthy foundation for the work of evangelism. People are invited into a fellowship where they see the gospel in flesh and blood, lived out in our relationships. This is the kind of fellowship where discipleship can happen.

Relevance and faithfulness: It is very important to create churches that are relevant to people outside of the church. Church planting is all about making the gospel relevant in any given context. But the desire for relevance can also become a stumbling block. We must never compromise the gospel in our search for relevance. When we wish to identify with the culture, we must be sure that our motivation originates from the right attitudes. We can have the greatest dreams and plans, but if we're not truly humble and faithful in our attitude

[22] Proverbs 16:8

[23] 2 Corinthians 12:9

toward the Word of God, we are sure to fail.[22] Our desire to be relevant to our audience must never replace an uncompromising faithfulness to the gospel and honesty about what it truly costs to follow Christ.

You can't get away from it – family comes first: The church is described as the family of God, and a well-functioning family is one of the best role models for a new fellowship. Our families need to be in the position to demonstrate how we grow in the Word of God, how we speak grace and truth to each other, and how to love our neighbors in word and action. But if our family situation is filled with strife, there is a good chance that the church plant will be, also.

Devotion to the church is not an excuse for troubles in the family—a church planter can never hide behind his or her church activities. A healthy church planter is a healthy husband and father, wife and mother. An ailing marriage and a poorly functioning family can never be justified by our commitment to the ministry.

These are some of the lessons we've learned along the way; in M4 these and many other issues will be covered. You will be challenged to reflect on your own life and ministry and to go through different processes together as the core group of your church-planting team. If you really want to benefit from this process, you have to dare to open up and be honest with each other. Paul teaches us:

> "'My grace is sufficient for you, for my power is made perfect in weakness.' Therefore I will boast all the more gladly about my weaknesses, so that Christ's power may rest on me." [23]

If we want to possess the power that God wants to give us, we must be humble, obedient and submissive to the one who has "all the power on heaven and on earth." This is where everything starts.

"All authority in heaven and on
earth has been given to me."

Master

M1 -
MASTER
-All authority has been given to me

M1-0

INTRODUCTION – BY ØIVIND AUGLAND

"God blesses the mega church in Korea and the house church in China. Hold to your models loosely and to Jesus firmly." - Ed Stetzer

"There is not a square inch of the entire creation about which Jesus Christ does not cry out, 'This is mine! This belongs to me!'" - Abraham Kuyper

"All authority on heaven and on earth has been given to me."[24] This is the first line of the Great Commission. It all starts with God's power and with God's commissioning. The church is his dream and initiative. He says: "I will build my church."[25] The church is *his*. The church exists *for* him and *through* him. If you want to plant a new church, you need to know who has sent you and what you're called to. We believe that it is important to have a clear understanding of who God is—"The one who is given all authority"—and to recognize his call on what you're moving into.

We've learned that when things get tough in church planting, it is the call of God on our lives that carries us through. When you feel like giving up, when conflicts flare up on the team, when you've been disappointed by people and you don't see any growth, there is one thing that still stands: God has called you, and his promises are still true!

26. Proverbs 29:18

Others should also recognize the call of God on your life. Do you have leaders around you who recognize your call to start up a new church? What kind of relationship do you have with them— and do you listen to them?

Planting a church in Scandinavia or Europe today demands a long-term focus: to build up a viable fellowship or network of smaller groups can take four to seven years. It can happen in a shorter time as well, but we'd say that this is the time it normally takes. The authors of M4 agree that church planting is one of the most amazing things you can do, but we also know that it can be a major challenge that requires commitment and endurance.

It is important that you as a church planting team are accountable to someone outside of the process. It could be to a network, organization or church denomination. It should be natural to turn to the leadership in the mother church or find other trustworthy people who are able to follow up the team over time. It is essential to mobilize prayer support from the mother church, church network or other partners. These relationships are essential for every church planter or team.

Relationship is a key word within church planting. To build up a healthy new church, we have to start with building healthy relationships in the core team. In M1-3 Terje Dale writes about building up the core team in his introduction:

"Working together as a team can be a fantastic thing—full of dynamics, creativity and joy. But it can also be incredibly exhausting when heated debates and a lack of direction overtake the team. Psalm 133 describes a team that is good to be on and that bears good fruit: "How good and pleasant it is when God's people live together in unity!"

Investing time and effort in the church planting team by helping the group work well together is one of the most important things you can do during the first year of planting. The way the team learns to work together will form the DNA that will influence the church in the future.

"Where there is no revelation, people cast off restraint."[26] A clear vision is important for every church planting team. When God called the prophet Habakkuk he said: "Write down the revelation and make it plain on tablets so

[27] Habakkuk 2:2

[28] Luke 17:5-9

[29] Matthew 16:18

that whoever reads it may run with it."[27] If leaders don't have the courage to paint alternative pictures of what the future can look like, we end up repeating what we're already doing today. Planting a church deals with sharing a vision, a picture of the future that is not quite visible. Be bold and proclaim what God has called you to, and make it clear to the core team. It is essential to clarify and model your vision and core values—particularly in the early stages of the church planting process. Øystein Gjerme writes about this when he shares his experiences from planting the Salt Bergen Church.

As a church planter your leadership is based on your relationship with God, and you only learn to know him through obedience. Faith grows and develops through obedience.[28] I learned early on as a church planter that it's not about *me,* it's about *him*—the one who "has been given all authority on heaven and on earth" and who says, *"I will build my church."*[29]

M1-1

THE KINGDOM OF GOD AND HIS POWER – BY ØIVIND AUGLAND

M1-1-1   Introduction

When I was 23 I was hired by Randesund Free Church, located on the east side of the southern Norwegian city of Kristiansand. One of my main tasks was to plant a church in the community of Hånes, which is located just three kilometers away from the mother church.

My wife Linda and I had just gotten married, and we found a place to live in Hånes. We challenged people from the mother church to join us as part of the core team, and soon a group of 10-15 adults was formed. After we started up the work, members from the mother church would often ask us how we were doing. There were two particular questions we kept getting: "How many are you now?" and "Do you have any plans for a church building yet?"

We felt as if we had to prove the right of our existence by increasing in number each time we met, something we were actually working really hard on. But if we wanted to be a 'proper' church we'd have to have our own building! Remember I was just in my twenties and newly married – and then we had *four children in six years*. All this was challenging enough. But on top of all this I was responsible for the growth of a fledgling fellowship and was anxious that we weren't a 'proper' church because we didn't have our own church building!

I am very grateful for the advisors I had around me at that time. They believed in me and the call God had given me. They prayed for me, supported and encouraged me, and even gathered finances for me. They helped me ask myself the right questions: Who is *really* responsible for this church? Whose initiative was it, and who gives the growth? I've reflected on these questions a lot, and I still discuss them with other leaders and church planters today.

When planting a new fellowship it is important to keep the right focus. Jesus says: "I will build my church." It's his will to plant churches; it's his initiative and he takes part in the process. The church exists for him and through him. I needed to hear this from my advisors, and I discovered that even Jesus' disciples needed to hear the same thing: When Jesus was leaving them, he said: "All authority has

[30] Matthew 28:18

[31] Psalms 103:19f;
Daniel 4;
Revelation
11:5-19

[32] Psalms 104:29

[33] Job 34:14-15

[34] 2 Corinthians 5:19

[35] Revelation 11:5-19

[36] Romans 1:5

[37] Romans 15:17-19

been given to me." This is where it all starts: In God, in his commission, in him who has been given "all authority in heaven and on earth."

M1-1-2 God's initiative

M1-1-2-1 God's power and authority

When Jesus says to the disciples "All authority has been given to me on heaven and on earth"[30] it means that God is king of the universe with unrestricted authority for all eternity.[31] History is all about *his story*.

David says in the book of Psalms, "When you hide your face, they are terrified; when you take away their breath, they die and return to the dust."[32] Job understood the power of God's omnipotence as he said, "If it was his intention and he withdrew his spirit and breath, all humanity would perish together and mankind would return to the dust."[33]

God is sovereign, and he has taken the initiative to reconcile the whole world to himself.[34] With the sending of Jesus to this world the kingdom of God became near. God has a purpose with his actions in history: to place everything on the earth under his lordship. His will shall be done on earth.[35] When Paul describes his ministry, he says, "Through him we received grace and apostleship to call all the Gentiles to the obedience that comes from faith for his name's sake."[36]

This is what church planting is all about: to lead people in obedience to Christ so that their lives can honor his name. This is how Paul sums up his service in his letter to the Romans:

> "Therefore I glory in Christ Jesus in my service to God. I will not venture to speak of anything except what Christ has accomplished through me in leading the Gentiles to obey God by what I have said and done - by the power of signs and wonders, through the power of the Spirit of God. So from Jerusalem all the way around to Illyricum, I have fully proclaimed the gospel of Christ."[37]

We must never forget that we are called to lead people into obedience to God and his will. To do this, we must understand who God really is. My experience is that we as Christian leaders and church planters lead others based on the personal revelation and understanding we have of God.

[38] Revelation 1:4-6

M1-1-2-2 The ruler of the kings of the earth

It is interesting to see what John writes to the seven newly planted churches in the Book of Revelation. The churches had different challenges and problems; some of the challenges came from within the church and others came from outside pressure. John was sitting alone on the island of Patmos when he wrote. He was the last remaining disciple; most of the others had been killed for their faith—John himself had experienced many tests and trials. He greets the new churches and shows the focus that is necessary to have as leaders:

> "Grace and peace to you from him who is, and who was, and who is to come, and from the seven spirits befor2e his throne, and from Jesus Christ, who is the faithful witness, the firstborn from the dead, and the ruler of the kings of the earth. To him who loves us and has freed us from our sins by his blood and has made us to be a kingdom and priests to serve his God and Father - to him be glory and power forever and ever! Amen."[38]

Even when he was lonely and surrounded by challenges, John did not fall into self-pity. He had a number of chances to do so, but John knew God, and he knew where to go with his disappointments, wounds and pain: to Jesus.

When planting a church, we must understand *who* God is. The seven churches from the Book of Revelation experienced external pressure, misunderstandings and rejection; they were persecuted because they refused to submit to the Roman authorities. They needed to hear and understand that their God was "the King of all kings." What could the kings of the earth really do to them? They could do nothing but take their lives. Remember that He is "the firstborn from the dead." Death is overcome. "Jesus Christ is the faithful witness" that this is true.

As John continues to write he clarifies how God sees them: "highly beloved and freed from your sins." They must see themselves as part of "the eternal Kingdom" which will one day permeate this God-created world. They are priests before God and they have the right to come to Him in all matters. For they

[39] Matthew 16:18

[40] John 10:10

[41] Isaiah 9:7

[42] 2 Corinthians 4:4

[43] John 10:10

[44] John 12:31; Ephesians 3:1-13

belong to the one who has "the glory and the power in all eternity." This is John's introductory greeting; he begins with a proclamation of who God is and who they are in him. It is only after he had written this that he proceeds to correct and guide the young churches.

M1-1-2-3 I will build my church

He who is sovereign and all-powerful is the one who says: "I will build my church, and the gates of Hades will not overcome it."[39] At the age of twenty-three I was explained the importance of this verse:

I WILL: God takes the initiative. He cheers on the establishment of new fellowships and congregations. God desires to gather people from all tribes and tongues. He wants to see his Kingdom continuously expand to new cities and regions, to all social and ethnic groups in our nations. It is God who calls and equips us. He has everything we need to have life and have it to the full.[40] He has everything we need for the task that lay ahead of us.

I WILL BUILD: God not only takes the initiative, he also cares for the growth. God wants growth, he wants to build, and he wants expansion and development. "Of the greatness of his government and peace there will be no end."[41] My experience is that a lack of spiritual growth in a person's life can be blamed on a lack of personal obedience to God. God loves people, and he desires that all come to the knowledge of the truth.

I WILL BUILD MY CHURCH: It is Jesus' church. It's not *our* church or *my* church, it's *his* church. He is Lord and deserves to have a say in his church: we cannot be indifferent to how we build it and what we do with it. The calling and the purpose of the church are far too important to be determined just by people— we have to involve Jesus in the decisions we make for his church.

THE GATES OF HADES WILL NOT OVERCOME IT: Planting churches is to be on a conquering raid of love, bearing the message that God loves all people. Gates are not constructed for attack, but for the purpose of keeping some in and others out. "The gates of Hades" is a description of what the evil one does to "blind the minds of unbelievers, so that they cannot see the light of the gospel that displays the glory of Christ, who is the image of God."[42] The evil one is out "to steal and kill and destroy."[43] We have a mission to conquer and occupy the territories of the enemy. The prince of this world is defeated.[44] Jesus describes what happened as follows:

[45] Luke 11:17-23

[46] Psalms 127:1

[47] Ephesians 6:13 ff

"Jesus knew their thoughts and said to them: "Any kingdom divided against itself will be ruined, and a house divided against itself will fall. If Satan is divided against himself, how can his kingdom stand? I say this because you claim that I drive out demons by Beelzebul. Now if I drive out demons by Beelzebul, by whom do your followers drive them out? So then, they will be your judges. But if I drive out demons by the finger of God, then the kingdom of God has come upon you. "When a strong man, fully armed, guards his own house, his possessions are safe. But when someone stronger attacks and overpowers him, he takes away the armor in which the man trusted and divides up his plunder. "Whoever is not with me is against me, and whoever does not gather with me scatters."[45]

As a church planter it is important to understand this: To start a new fellowship in a culture, ethnic group or geographic area *is a declaration of war on the enemy.* Church planting must never be considered merely a human activity. We are truly doing a spiritual work: we work and pray, fighting in the power that God gives us. Prayer within the core team of the church-planting ministry is essential. Pray for the people, the schools, the institutions, and for all that is happening in the area. Pray for the expansion of God's kingdom. I remember that during my first years of church planting in Hånes we frequently went on prayer walks in the area – alone or together with others. We prayed for the presence of God in Hånes and that he would put an end to the increasing drug scene. We prayed for the schools, and committed ourselves to working on local boards and committees. Every house and every apartment was covered with prayer. Even people who weren't involved in the church planting team were mobilized in regular prayer for this work.

Church planting is giving all you've got in the knowledge that "Unless the LORD builds the house, the builders labor in vain."[46] Church planting is mobilizing a conquering people in full knowledge that the battle is lost before it even begins if it is not fought with the full armor of God.[47] As I heard somebody say once: "The world around us tells us to fight, get the victory and then rest. But in the kingdom of God the order is different: fight, rest – and then you get the victory." This is the paradoxical truth. God causes the growth, but he also has made

[48] Church: Greek *ekklesia* occurs in the New Testament 114 times, most often in the Pauline letters (61). In the gospels the word only occurs three times. It means "they who are chosen" and is translated as *church, congregation* or *community*. It is used in three primary ways: 1) *the universal church*: Matthew 16:18; Acts 20:28; Ephesians 1:22, 3:10, 3:21; 5:25-27; Colossians 1:18, 1:24;Revelation 22:17 (altogether 20 times); 2) *the congregation on each place* occurs 87 times: in a city (Acts 5:11, 8:1,13:1; 1 Corinthians 1:2 and other letter addresses, and the letters in Revelation 2-3); and in a larger area (Acts 9:31); 3) *the community in the homes* occurs four times (1 Corinthians 16:15; Romans 16:3-5; Colossians 4:15; Philemon 1:2).

[49] The Kingdom of God: Greek *basileia* occurs 141 times in the New Testament, mostly in Matthew (41 times) and Luke (39 times). It is only used 13 times in Paul's letters.

[50] Hirsh, Allan and Frost, Michael. The Shaping of the Things to Come. Edinburgh: Hendrickson Publishers, 2001; Frost, Michael. Exiles: Living Missionally in a Post-Christian Culture. Edinburgh: Hendrickson Publishers, 2006; Hirsch, Allan and Frost, Michael.ReJesus: A Wild Messiah for a Missional Church. Edinburgh: Hendrickson Publishers, 2009.

[51] Warren, Robert. Being Human, Being Church. London: Marshall Pickering, 1995.

himself dependent on His people to extend his kingdom on earth.

M1-1-2-4 The kingdom of God is the goal – not the church

There are two terms from the New Testament that are important to understand as church planters: *church*[48] and *the kingdom of God*[49]. The word *church* occurs mostly in Paul's epistles, while the expression *the kingdom of God* occurs most frequently in the gospels. Today there is a tendency to emphasize the gospel texts in the church planting literature.[50]

Jesus is our role model. We are called to follow Jesus, and when we do, he sends us out in mission. On our mission we get people saved and then disciple them to follow Jesus. Disciples then gather together and new churches are formed.

JESUS – COMMISSIONING – SAVING PEOPLE – DISCIPLING – CHURCH

Church planting starts with obedience, mission and discipleship. We are not called to build his church but to make disciples and extend his kingdom. When this happens, *he* will build his church. This can be a corrective to a narrow focus where the goal has been churches, often defined as programs, activities, and a building program. In our European context *church* has often been defined in the following manner:

CHURCH = BUILDING AND PASTOR + MONEY TO PAY FOR THE BUILDING AND PASTOR[51]

We believe that it is necessary to find a balance between thinking about the kingdom of God and our focus on church; we also need a balance between the gospel accounts and the epistles. A church is not merely an organic unit; it soon takes on elements of an organization.

A church is both dynamic and static.[52] With the backdrop of our own church planting stories, we see that it is crucial that from the very beginning growth comes from getting people saved and discipled. The kingdom of God is our goal, not the church itself. It is exactly this that's been God's dream from the beginning.

M1-1-3   The dream of God

When Linda and I got married we moved into the area where we were planting the church. We rented a small apartment above a double garage and after a short while we started to dream of having our own house and a permanent place to live. I'm sure a lot of young couples have dreamt of getting their own home, a home they can start to decorate, furnish and make into whatever they want, of a place they can retreat to, where they can disconnect from the world, be the lord of their own home. Have you ever had thoughts like this? Anyway, we had a dream like this.

God also has a dream – a deep longing in his heart since the dawn of time. It is a dream he will see fulfilled one day. His dream is to build a house that can serve as his dwelling place on earth. It is a dream of forming a place according to his own plans where he can be the Lord of the house and do whatever he wants. It will be a home, a dwelling place that he can fill with his desires and his presence.

M1-1-3-1   The tent of meeting

The history of salvation testifies to the dream and longing of God. It started with a tabernacle – a "tent of meeting." When Moses left Egypt and met God up on the mountain he was given the following mission: "Then have them make a sanctuary for me, and I will dwell among them. Make this tabernacle and all its furnishings exactly like the pattern that I will show you."[53]

God explained in detail how they should build it. God was not indifferent to how things were done; he had an opinion about it. He wanted to explain what his house and dwelling place should be like.[54]

When the tent of meeting was completed, God had a place to dwell among the people whom he loved. We can read about how the presence of God rested over the tent of meeting. God was present in the midst of his people.

[52] Schwartz, Christian and Logan, Robert E. Natural Church Development: A Guide to Eight Essential Qualities of Healthy Churches. 1996.

[53] Exodus 25:8-9

[54] Exodus 25:28

[55] Exodus 40:35-38

[56] Acts 7:45-46

[57] 1 Kings 8:1

[58] 1 Kings 9:3

[59] John 1:14

"Moses could not enter the tent of meeting because the cloud had settled on it and the glory of the LORD filled the tabernacle. In all the travels of the Israelites, whenever the cloud lifted from above the tabernacle, they would set out; but if the cloud did not lift, they did not set out – until the day it lifted. So the cloud of the LORD was over the tabernacle by day, and fire was in the cloud by night, in the sight of all the Israelites during all their travels."[55]

Through his nearness and presence in his dwelling place, God led his people. The hope and salvation of Israel was that God was present in his dwelling place. He showed the way. Later in the history of the people of Israel we again see how God fulfilled his dream by building his dwelling place among his people.

M1-1-3-2   The temple

When Peter explains what happened on the day of Pentecost, he speaks of the building of the Temple: "[The tent of meeting] remained in the land until the time of David, who enjoyed God's favor and asked that he might provide a dwelling place for the God of Jacob. But it was Solomon who built a house for him."[56] In the first book of Kings we can read King Solomon's prayer: "I have indeed built a magnificent temple for you, a place for you to dwell forever."[57] And we read how the Lord's Spirit, presence and glory filled the temple. And God reassures Solomon that he is delighted in his work. "The LORD said to him: "I have heard the prayer and plea you have made before me; I have consecrated this temple, which you have built, by putting my Name there forever. My eyes and my heart will always be there.""[58] Now God once again had a place to dwell among his people, a resting place. But the people of Israel looked forward to the time when God would build his dwelling place *in* the people and *of* the people.

M1-1-3-3   He made his dwelling among us

And so the day finally came: God took the initiative and sent his son Jesus Christ to the world. "The Word became flesh and made his dwelling among us. We have seen his glory, the glory of the one and only Son, who came from the Father, full of grace and truth."[59] And so God's dream was fulfilled again. He came and built his house among the people—not in a tent of meeting or in a temple, but within the person of Jesus Christ. The word from the Psalms was fulfilled: "Surely his salvation is near those who fear him that his glory may dwell in our land. Love and faithfulness meet together; righteousness and peace kiss each other."[60] His glory was made visible for us through Jesus Christ and it was recognized by grace and truth.

[60] Psalms 85:9-10

[61] 2 Corinthians 6:16

[62] Ephesians 2:19-22

M1-1-3-4 Built for a dwelling place for the Spirit of the LORD

But God had an even greater plan. He would dwell not just in a body, the body of Jesus Christ, but he would form a new dwelling place—a house, not built of solid rock but of malleable stones, living stones. "For we are the temple of the living God." As God has said: "I will live with them and walk with them, and I will be their God, and they will be my people."[61] This is also what Paul was teaching the church of Ephesus:

> "...You are no longer foreigners and strangers, but fellow citizens with God's people and also members of his household, built on the foundation of the apostles and prophets, with Christ Jesus himself as the chief cornerstone. In him the whole building is joined together and rises to become a holy temple in the Lord. And in him you too are being built together to become a dwelling in which God lives by his Spirit."[62]

God still has a dream to make his presence known here on earth—not in a tent or a temple but through a people who is called and consecrated for him. A people that have one goal: to give praise and honor to him; to be a people who are willing to be built together into a dwelling place exactly as he wants it, where he may rest and present himself to the entire world—a dwelling place built up of people who have opened their hearts to him and allowed him to be the lord over his handiwork.

We must never degrade the call to plant churches by making it only about meetings, activities and programs. Church planting is first and foremost about fulfilling the dream of God. God's longing is to find a people, a group of individuals in every village, city, culture and ethnic group who are willing to become his dwelling place. God longs for people he can do his will through, who are light and salt in a world ruled by darkness and decay. This is the reason why we should ask *how* we can build rather than *what* we can build. It matters how

[63] John 1:14

[64] Acts 2:46

[65] Acts 2:1 – 8:4, in particular 5:14-16

[66] 8:4-25

[67] 10:1-11, 18

we build his house. Ephesians 3 to 6 explains how life in God's house should be lived:

...Live a life worthy of the calling you have received. Be completely humble and gentle; be patient, bearing with one another in love. Make every effort to keep the unity of the Spirit through the bond of peace" (4:1-3). We must "put off falsehood and speak truthfully to your neighbor, for we are all members of one body" (4:25). It includes the way we talk: "Do not let any unwholesome talk come out of your mouths, but only what is helpful for building others up according to their needs, that it may benefit those who listen" (4:29). It is about forgiving each other: "Be kind and compassionate to one another, forgiving each other, just as in Christ God forgave you!" (4:32). We must "walk in the way of love, just as Christ loved us and gave himself up for us" (5:2). In all things we must be "speaking the truth in love" (4:15).

These verses are a practical expression of his glory made visible through people who are living in "grace and truth"[63] in and through their fellowship. Church planting is to realize God's dream: that in every geographic place, culture and ethnic group there dwells a people who desire to live according to what he says. In this way will many more new people believe and become disciples when they see "how they love one another."[64]

The power of the Word is made visible when people accept it and allow their lives to be influenced by it. This becomes clear to us in a special way when we read the Book of Acts.

M1-1-4   The church of God

M1-1-4-1   The church in the Book of Acts

In the Book of Acts Luke sums up the progress of church planting through three growth phases. He describes what happens in, around, and beyond Jerusalem, Antioch, and Ephesus. All three places are characterized by growth that starts in the city center that leads to the multiplication of new churches and fellowships in the surrounding areas. It started in Jerusalem with a period of growth within the Jewish community.[65] The first Christians were accused of having "filled Jerusalem with their teaching" (5:28). After some time the revival broke out in Samaria;[66] Peter then receives a vision that leads him to the house of Cornelius, baptizing him and his household.[67] The gospel then spreads to the metropolis of

Antioch, which becomes a new center for missions.[68] Paul and Barnabas are sent out by the leading of The Holy Spirit. We read that "the churches were strengthened in faith and grew daily in numbers."[69] Afterward churches were planted in Salamis,[70] Paphos,[71] Perga,[72] Antioch-Pisidia,[73] Iconium,[74] Lystra,[75] Derbe[76] and Attalia.[77]

Everywhere the believers gathered churches were planted. "Paul and Barnabas appointed elders for them in each church and, with prayer and fasting, committed them to the Lord, in whom they had put their trust."[78] The movement spread to both Philippi[79] and Thessalonica.[80] Paul stayed in Thessalonica only a few weeks, but a new church was founded through his preaching and the demonstration of the gospel. At this time Paul says: "So we cared for you. Because we loved you so much, we were delighted to share with you not only the gospel of God but our lives as well."[81] Churches arose in Berea,[82] Athens[83] and Corinth.[84] A church was planted soon after in Ephesus[85] and a new base for missions to Europe and Asia was established.

What we see in the Book of Acts is the natural expansion of the gospel. Luke sums up and describes the three phases with the following words:

JERUSALEM: "So the word of God spread. The number of disciples in Jerusalem increased rapidly, and a large number of priests became obedient to the faith."[86]

ANTIOCH: "But the word of God continued to spread and flourish."[87]

EPHESUS: "This way the word of the Lord spread widely and grew in power."[88]

Steve Timmis and Tim Chester in *The Crowded House* talk about being "Gospel centered,"[89]and this is precisely what we have seen in the book of Acts. It is the gospel of the kingdom of God that is expanding. The gospel will spread when the Word of God touches people and the number of disciples grows. The same thing that happened in the book of Acts is happening on all five continents today. Europe is the continent least affected by a visible expansion of the kingdom of God; but if we look closely, there are many glimpses of light here as well. God is doing something new in Europe.

[68] 11:20

[69] 16:5

[70] 13:5

[71] 13:9-12

[72] 13:13

[73] 13:16-41

[74] 14:1

[75] 14:8-19

[76] 14:20-21

[77] 14:25

[78] 14:23

[79] 16:11

[80] 17:1-4

[81] 1 Thessalonians 2:8

[82] Acts 17:10-12

[83] 17:14-34

[84] 18:1-11

[85] 19:1ff

[86] Acts 6:7

[87] Acts 12:24

[88] Acts 19:20

[89] Timmis, Steve, Chester, Tim: Total church, a radical reshaping around gospel and community. Wheaton, Ill: Crossway Books, 2008.

[90] Schindler,
Dietrich.
www.feg.de

[91] Crebs, Reinhold.
www.jugonet.de;
www.churchnight.de

[92] Anzenberger,
Raphael.
www.1pour10000.fr

[93] Robinson Martin.
Together in Mission;
http://bit.ly/togMis

[94] Dyhr, Peter.
www.ecpn.com

[95] Greg, Pete and
Blackwell, David.
24-7 Prayer
Manual, 2008
(3ed edition)

M1-1-4-2 Church planting today – it's on the move

Though evangelical churches are still in stagnation in most places in Europe, there are still many signs of change. In Germany, the German Covenant Church is planting one new church every month, and their goal is to see one hundred new churches planted before 2015.[90] The Lutheran Church in Wurttemberg, Germany is actively working within the youth culture in their area. They gather thousands of young people to their meetings, and are training leaders to plant new fellowships.[91] In France, leaders from all denominations and organizations have gathered around a strategy to see hundreds of new churches established, with regional centers for training church planters established in many places now.[92] In England hundreds of churches are planted every year and most churches and church networks have a clear strategy for church planting.[93] The same thing is happening in Holland and Portugal: through the European Church Planting Network several hundred churches and fellowships have been planted the last five years.[94] The largest trend we see in Europe today is immigrant churches, with hundreds of them being planted in Europe each month.

M1-1-4-3 Obedience – the great challenge

The landscape ahead of us is more challenging and complex than ever. Cultures differ from city to countryside, even from city to city, town to town. From Hamburg to Prague, from Latvia to Portugal, from Norway to Italy the differences in culture and peoples are enormous.

I once talked to a church planter and asked him where he learned to do church planting. His simple answer was: "I haven't really been taught that much. I've just tried to follow the instructions Jesus has given me and to be obedient to him. And it's worked so far." I believe we could learn a lot from the experience of others—and we need to. But what is most important in the times ahead is that we are obedient to the one who is:

"The head of his church." And to let our "feeble, whispered, faithless prayer invokes a thunderous, resounding, bone-shaking great 'Amen!' from countless angels, from hero's of the faith, from Christ himself. And he is the original dreamer, the ultimate winner."[95]

Dare to dream with the one who so loved the world that he gave his life for it. I am convinced that we will see many new, vibrant fellowships that dare to cross all boundaries, experiment with new forms and expressions of doing church, and are ready to do anything "so that by all possible means they might save some."[96]

[96] 1 Corinthians 9:22

M1-2

THE CHURCH PLANTER – BY ØIVIND AUGLAND

97 Hopkins, Bob and Mary, *Church Planting Coaching Manual.* Sheffield: Anglican Church Planting Initiative, 2003.

M1-2-1   Introduction

I felt really young when we planted our first church, which was in the community of Hånes in Kristiansand, Norway. Most of the other team members were older than me. We had a call to plant a church but we didn't have a whole lot of experience. Even though I was young and I didn't really see myself as a strong leader, I noticed that my thoughts, words, and opinions meant a lot to the people on the team. We shared the same vision for a new church, but it was still me who was the vision-bearer. There were a number of people in leadership, but they all looked to me when decisions had to be made.

In the first phase of a church planting work, the roll of the church planter and vision-bearer is crucial. This phase requires you to take initiative and to give clear direction to the process.[97] It doesn't mean that the leader has to take all the initiative, but the leader has to *lead*. The following statement illustrates how I see my responsibility as a Christian leader: "to recognize what God is doing in the body of the church and provide direction for it." As the leader I had to dare to give direction, because we couldn't do everything everyone on the team wanted to do. We shouldn't do everything that comes to our minds. Leaders must be bold enough to say yes or no. We have to keep in mind the call and where we want to go: What kind of church are we called to be? What is our vision? What is our model? Who are we called to reach?

I also discovered that it was important how I lived my life. My family and I were actually establishing the culture for the new fellowship. The culture of a new fellowship doesn't come by chance; it is formed through the life we live together as a core group. As a leader I have to dare to lead in these things as well. When I look back I can see that a number of the values Linda and I had when we first planted the church are still part of the church today: openness, generosity, hospitality and flexibility. Even without realizing it at the time, we affected the culture and life we find in the church today.

This illustrates how important it is that I as a leader choose to live in open and accountable relationships with others. If the life of the leader affects the church so much, we can expect that a leader's more unfavorable qualities can also affect the church. This happens when we don't live in open and mutually accountable relationships with others.

One day one of my older co-leaders came to me and asked: "Have you really experienced the full depth of the grace of God?" I wondered what he meant by that. He began to reflect on my preaching which he found a bit demanding and legalistic. This led to an open and honest discussion in the leadership about this, and I received teaching and input from them that I would never want to live without.

A call has both an *inner* and *outer* dimension. An inner call is the conviction that one has heard from God; an outer call is the recognition by others of that inner call. In relation to a doctoral thesis Jan Inge Jenssen wrote at the University of Agder in Kristiansand, I was asked to interview nearly 120 church planters in Norway.[98] I spoke with each of them for an hour or two. During these interviews I could easily distinguish between those who were driven by a clear call and those who doubted their own work and reasons for doing it. While talking to them I realized how crucial it is that leaders and pastors confirm the call a church planter has on his or her life.

Planting a church in Europe is a long-term project. When we started the church in Hånes I asked the core team members to commit to the work for at least three years. I can see now that this is one of the main reasons why we succeeded. It gave us predictability, peace, and clarity so that we were able to build together. Our experience in Scandinavia tells us that it normally takes about four to seven years to build up a healthy church. But there will be individual differences in how long it takes from church to church, and whether the work occurs in an urban or rural area.

I will be addressing these themes below. It is important that you reflect on these themes and act on whatever questions they might stir up in you.

I have also included "possible characteristics of a church planter." This is meant to be the basis for prayer and personal reflection. It can be used as a tool to evaluate the call God has given you to be a church planter. It can also be used on your team as a basis for discussion about the call and skills needed to plant in a new fellowship on a church planting team.

[98] Jenssen, Jan Inge. *Does the degree of redundancy in social networks influence the success of business start-ups?* 2002.

[99] http://www.merriam-webster.com/dictionary/call. Accessed 04.09.2012. The words *call* and *calling* are similar, though *call* carries more the connotation of divine origin or initiative, while *calling* has more to do with the vocation or life work that is a response to a divine call (See ibid, *calling*). In this book we use the terms according to the context.

[100] Donders, Paul Christian. *Creative Life Planning: Discover Your Calling, Develop Your Potential.* Kristiansand, Norway. Sidevedside forlag, 2008.

[101] Whitmore, John. *Coaching for Performance.* San Diego: Pfeiffer, 2002.

[102] Donders, Paul Christian and Jaap, Ketelaar. *Value Centred Leadership in Church and Organisations.* Argyll: Xpand 2011 (The entire leadership profile can be ordered online at www.xpand.eu).

M1-2-2 Commission and call

Call is a word we haven't seen much of the last ten years, but is now seen both within and outside of the church context. A call is "a divine vocation or strong inner prompting to a particular course of action."[99] The demands, changes, and opportunities we are surrounded with in our daily lives force us to be conscious of how we make use of our resources, skills, talents and time. I need to be clearer about what I want to use my life for. I have to take control of my life, or else the demands of the world will end up controlling me.[100] In a time when the accessible amount of knowledge is doubled every third of fourth year, we are constantly forced to relate to new impulses. John Whitmore expresses the situation like this:

> "When most of what we know is constantly changing, we must accept the responsibility of our own life both physically and mentally in order to survive. We have to take care of ourselves because no one else will do so in a world where everybody has to deal with change."[101]

We have to take responsibility to form our own lives and use our talents and skills in a meaningful way to serve the kingdom of God and the people around us in the best possible way.

To keep control of your life in a world where the amount of change and options are constantly increasing, people today need to be made accountable for the values they hold and the call they have on their lives. As a church planter and leader it is good to reflect on the following questions. [102]

Please use the scale to evaluate yourself. 1 means that the statement is not valid or appropriate, and 5 means the statement is a perfect description of your situation.

○ ○ ○ ○ ○
1 2 3 4 5

I am aware of who and what has helped to form my life.

○ ○ ○ ○ ○
1 2 3 4 5

I have evaluated and reflected upon the different phases of my life.

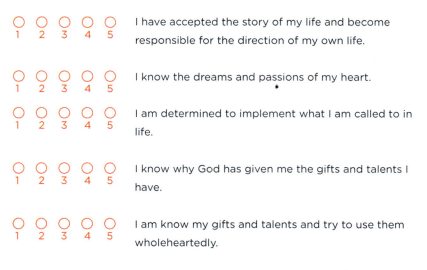

O O O O O   I have accepted the story of my life and become
1 2 3 4 5   responsible for the direction of my own life.

O O O O O   I know the dreams and passions of my heart.
1 2 3 4 5

O O O O O   I am determined to implement what I am called to in
1 2 3 4 5   life.

O O O O O   I know why God has given me the gifts and talents I
1 2 3 4 5   have.

O O O O O   I am know my gifts and talents and try to use them
1 2 3 4 5   wholeheartedly.

[103] John 18:37

[104] Matthew 26:39

A healthy self-consciousness and an understanding of who you are and what you are called to are important when leading others in the planting of a new fellowship. In the conversation with Pontius Pilate Jesus clearly stated his call:

"You are king, then!" said Pilate. Jesus answered, "You say that I am king. In fact, the reason I was born and came into the world is to testify to the truth. Everyone on the side of truth listens to me."[103]

Jesus was fully confident in his call and prepared to stand by it, even though it would cost him everything: "Going a little farther, he fell with his face to the ground and prayed, "My Father, if it is possible, may this cup be taken from me. Yet not as I will, but as you will."[104] Paul and Peter were both confident in their respective calls, having received them when they met the living Jesus Christ.

[105] Malm, Magnus. *Vägvisere, en bok om kristent lederskap.* Uppsala: EFS forlag, 1990.

[106] 1 Corinthians 1:9

[107] See footnote on the usage of call and calling, above.

I was quite young when I read Magnus Malm's book: "Pathfinders – a book on Christian leadership.[105] It became an important book to me. Malm writes that our main call is to live in a relationship with Jesus Christ. "God is faithful, he who has called you into fellowship with his Son, Jesus Christ our Lord."[106] Our call is first of all to him, and from our encounter with him we are sent out in service. This is the point we have tried to emphasize in this first chapter: we lead based on our revelation of God's character and our relationship with him. From this relationship we are sent out in service and if your ministry vanishes and the church planting doesn't succeed, so what? Your initial call still stands, which is *to live in relationship with God and to seek his face.*

I am convinced that, when speaking of call and church planting, you as the leader must know that God has led you into the work. When challenges arrive in the planting process, God's call is what carries you through. When you feel like giving up, when there are conflicts in the team, when people disappoint you and there's little growth, there is only one thing left: God has called you, and his promises are still true.

When I speak to people involved with church planting I learn that calls can vary quite a lot. Some people just want to work on a team to support the call-bearers; they want to serve others with the talents have as a way to be committed to a vision that burns in their hearts also. They may also see the new fellowship as a great opportunity to invite their non-Christian friends to. Others have a clear, independent call to a work on a specific church-planting team. These are all legitimate reasons to plant a church. The fact that motives and reasons for planting a church differ from person to person emphasizes the need for a leader to have a clear call and a long-term commitment to the work that is about to start.

By buying a house in Hånes, I sent a clear signal as a leader about my calling[107] and long-term commitment to the church planting work we were doing in the area. This was important to the people involved in the early stages of the church plant—It made them more whole-hearted in the work.

In my church-planting networks, we often talk about having both an *inner* and *outer* call. An *outer call* is recognition and confirmation from others about your call and gifts. I believe it is important to have an outer call that is confirmed by others. I've met people with a strong call on their lives, but who've received little or no support from the leaders around them—or haven't had anyone who's recognized that they're ready to work as a church planter or that they're even gifted for church planting. Under such circumstances it is important to stop and think and ask some questions. I write more below about why it is important to be accountable to someone during a planting process. It begins with being willing to reflect on your call with someone you trust—someone you are willing to listen to and take advice from.

On the other hand, I've also observed at different times leaders of church denominations and organizations who have held back young people who are obviously equipped with both call and giftings for church planting. This may be due to their own fears, bad experiences or lack of experience with church planting. Unhealed wounds and disappointments in church leaders can be effective hindrances to anything new and inventive. These leaders seem to "understand it all" and "explain everything", but they lack the passion and vision needed to release people around them into pioneer work.

M1-2-3 Equipping and personality

M1-2-3-1 Equipping[108] and personality

Not all of us are called to plant a church, but many of us can be part of a church planting team. By this we mean that not everyone is equipped with the gifts *to be the leader* or to *carry the vision* of a church planting work. At the same time we are convinced that church planting is a team effort that gives many kinds of people the opportunity to participate. The Methodist priest Leif Jacobsen wrote his doctoral thesis on leadership in the church-planting context.[109] After studying fifty church-planting ministries in more than ten denominations, he concluded, "A trained, structured and well-functioning leadership is an important success criterion for a new church. It is also documented that leaders with a certain type of personality are better church planters than others."[110]

Church planting literature takes the personality and equipping of the church planter seriously.[111] The Adventists have developed their own manual for church planting in Europe used to train and appoint church planting teams.[112] The German Covenant Church considers the

[108] *Equipping:* (noun) the act of equipping (as with weapons in preparation for war). In the Christian context, this term has come to refer to the gifts, abilities, talents, skills and experiences God has given an individual to accomplish the call or vocation he has given that individual. See http://www. thefreedictionary.com/ equipping (accessed 04.09.2012).

[109] Jacobsen S Leif. *The leadership factor in church planting projects in Norway from 1990 to 2000.* Virginia Beach: Regent University, 2005.

[110] Ibid, p 132.

[111] Malphurs, Aubrey. *Planting Growing Churches for the 21st Century: A Comprehensive Guide for New Churches and Those Desiring Renewal,* 2nd ed. Grand Rapids, MI, Baker Books, 1998. And *Advanced Strategic Planning: A New Model for Church and Ministry Leaders.* Grand Rapids, MI, Baker Books, 1999.

[112] Roenfelt Peter and Walker Philip. *Church planting manual 2002* and *Empowering Church planters through coaching;* 2002.

[113] Schindler, Dietrich. *Church Planting Multiplication in the Evangelical Free Church of Germany* (Lecture notes, DAWN Forum 2010).

[114] Addison Steve. *How to know if you should plant a church.* Church Resource Ministries Australia, 1993.

appointment of church planters very important when they are in the process of planting a new church.[113] Many denominations and organizations use various tools when they appoint new leaders and equip them. We believe that it is healthy to test your calling by reflecting on your gifts, personality and equipping. It may be useful to take a DISC personality profile from Persolog or use the Myers-Briggs Type Indicator (MBTI) in this process of reflection.

M1-2-3-2 Your call and equipping

The simple questions that follow may help you to reflect on your calling and your equipping. The questions are taken from Steve Addison's booklet «How to know if you should plant a church».[114] The questionnaire below is slightly edited. Please evaluate and rank yourself by numbers in each category based on your own experiences in ministry. And when you do so, please write down some specific examples of your behavior to validate your rating. You can use this assessment in dialog with the team or someone close to you (mentor, coach, pastor etc.). Let them go through your scores to make comments and give feedback.

1: Never 2: Rarely 3: Sometimes 4: Often 5: Always

○ ○ ○ ○ ○
1 2 3 4 5

Ability to create a vision: I have the ability to see clearly what direction God wants to lead my work, and I've been able to guide others in the same direction. Give specific examples.

○ ○ ○ ○ ○
1 2 3 4 5

Intrinsically motivated: I have the ability to implement and complete tasks well, despite financial restrictions, hard work and the investment of my time—without being closely supervised by others. Give specific examples.

○ ○ ○ ○ ○
1 2 3 4 5

Ministry ownership: I have the ability to inspire co-laborers so they are motivated to complete the work we do together and pursue our mutual goals. Give specific examples.

○ ○ ○ ○ ○
1 2 3 4 5

Relating to those outside the church: I have the ability to form good relationships with people outside of the church and convey the gospel to them in a way they can understand. Give specific examples.

○ ○ ○ ○ ○
1 2 3 4 5
Spousal unity (if relevant): My husband/wife or fiancée understands, accepts and supports my commitment to plant a new church and wants to stand by me in the work. Give specific examples.

○ ○ ○ ○ ○
1 2 3 4 5
Ability to build relationships: I am able to build good relationships with others and am sensitive to their needs. Give specific examples.

○ ○ ○ ○ ○
1 2 3 4 5
Growth in the church: I have a strong commitment to my church, and desire to see the kingdom of God and the church increase in numbers. Give specific examples.

○ ○ ○ ○ ○
1 2 3 4 5
Contextual and cultural understanding: I am sensitive to the culture that we are planting in and understand the needs of the people we are reaching out to with the gospel. I have an ability to create services to meet their needs. Give specific examples.

○ ○ ○ ○ ○
1 2 3 4 5
Release gifts and ministry in others: I have shown the ability to gather, train, coach and support others in identifying and utilizing their gifts and ministries. Give specific examples.

○ ○ ○ ○ ○
1 2 3 4 5
Flexible and adaptable: I have the ability to adapt to sudden changes and unforeseen incidents and use them for my benefit. Give specific examples.

○ ○ ○ ○ ○
1 2 3 4 5
Building a cohesive team/group: I have the ability to gather individuals into a committed and meaningful team ministry. I am able to help them solve conflicts when they occur. Give specific examples.

○ ○ ○ ○ ○
1 2 3 4 5
Endurance: I have the ability to face setbacks, disappointments and defeats without giving up or pulling back. Give specific examples.

○ ○ ○ ○ ○
1 2 3 4 5
Faith: I am convinced that God is calling me to start a new church and that he will provide me with everything I needed to complete the task. Give specific examples.

[115] Murray, Stuart and Wilkinson-Heys. Anne. *Hope from the Margins - New Ways of Being Church*. Cambridge, UK: Grove Books, 2000 (p 4-5).

[116] Neighbour, Ralph W. *Where Do We Go From Here? A Guidebook for the Cell Group Church*. Houston, TX: TOUCH publication, 2000. Beckham, William A. *The Second Reformation*. Houston, TX: TOUCH publication, 1997. Comiskey, Joel. *Home Cell Group Explosion: How Your Small Group Can Grow and Multiply*. Houston, TX: TOUCH publication, 2002; Comiskey, Joel. *Planting churches that reproduce: Starting network of simple Churches*. Lima OH: CCS publishing, 2009.

[117] Simson, Wolfgang. *Hjem som forandrer verden*. Grimerud: Prokla Media, 2006; Kreider, Larry. *House Church Networks: A Church for a New Generation*. Lititz, PA: House to House Publications, 2001.

[118] www.hillsong.com. See also www.hillsong.co.uk.

[119] www.redeemercitytocity.com

[120] Surratt, Geoff, Ligon , Greg and Bird, Varren. *The Multi-Site Church Revolution*. Grand Rapids: Zondervan, 2011.

[121] Cole, Neil. *Organic Church: Growing Faith Where Life Happens*. West Sussex: John Wiley & Sons, 2005. See also the website: www.simplechurch.eu

[122] Breen, Mike and Hopkins, Bob. *Cluster - Creative Mid-Sized Missional*. Sheffield: ACPI, 2009; Stetzer, Ed. *Planting Missional Churches*. Nashville, TN: Broadman & Holman Publishers, 2006; Hirsch, Allan. *The Forgotten Ways*. Grand Rapids: Brazos Press, 2006.

[123] Halter Hugh and Smay, Matt. *DNA - The Gathered and Scattered Church*. Grand Rapids: Zondervan, 2010.

M1-2-4 What are you called to plant?

M1-2-4-1 Different models for church planting

Many of the new churches planted in Europe during the 70s, 80s and 90s were "clones" of what already existed.[115] Fortunately, church planting today is constantly being expressed in new ways. As time progresses we will see an even greater variety of models and methods for church planting.

Even though M4 does not present a model for church planting or a special way for doing it, we don't mean to suggest that a systematic approach to your work is useless. We believe it is important for you to choose a model to work by so you are able to stay focused on the kind of church you want to plant. For some of you, a church-planting model can be determined by the context you are working in, while others may be able to choose more freely. M4 raises the questions that will help you think through the alternatives. Should it be a local church or a network fellowship? Will it be a cell-based [116] or a house church model[117] that will be the best in your situation? If your focus is on a large urban area, maybe you can look at the larger churches and networks such as Hillsong[118] or Redeemer[119] for inspiration? Do you have a dream for a multi-site church? [120] Is the model an organic movement? [121] Are you focused on missional fellowships[122] or something in-between? [123] Your job is to clarify the specific expression of church you see for your church plant, which may be different than any other church plant.

Our experience tells us that the relation between church-planting success and the choice of a church-planting model goes something like this: the model you choose is actually secondary; what *is* important is that you be true to the vision you have and what you see in the future. A lot of churches are impulse-driven, meaning that they follow the newest church-planting impulses and think they have to change their strategy, model and method when they see what others are doing in other places. But we believe that it is more important to have a clear vision, be faithful to it, stick to it, and go for it. You can use the new impulses for inspiration at the beginning of your work, utilizing whatever serves your choice of direction—and that serves what God has called you to build. We are convinced that as time goes on, church planting will be even more varied in both form and expression than what we've seen the past ten years. God is creative! If we are to be reflections of him we need to embrace an even more creative expression of church planting so we can reach the full breadth of the population of our nations. Be creative at the beginning, but then stick to the model you chose in the beginning!

A lot has been written about church planting methods, and many methods have been tested and implemented. Different methods are developed to meet differing contexts: neighborhoods differ (inner-city center, rural, mixed-ethnic cultures), people differ (spiritually mature, unreached, rebellious), and church planters differ (evangelist, teacher, counselor, musician, etc.). Here are some of the models that have been used:[124]

M1-2-4-2 The mother-daughter method
This method is based on the scenario where an established church plants one or more new churches. Usually this means that the church has to give up some of its members who leave to help plant a new, independent church. The method can be used in many different ways:

Elders-district method: In a district where several of the members of a church live, a long-term plan is enacted to develop an independent church in that district. The church appoints elders or leaders from the church members who live in the area, and who will lead the process of becoming an independent church. Thus a certain organizational structure is planned into the church-planting process from the very beginning.

District-worker method: You hire a person to build up a new church in a new area of the city or district. It is important that this person is free to recruit members from the mother church to help with the work—and who might even become members of the new church.

Team method: A team of volunteers is challenged and called to plant a new church in a new area of the city/district. The team should consist of people equipped with different spiritual gifts. The pastor or another person from the

[124] A more extended documentation on diffrent models and methodes of churchplanting you can find in the book *Global Church Planting: Biblical Principles and Best Practices for Multiplication.* Ott, Craig and Wilson, Gene. Grand Rapids: Baker Academic, 2011.

mother church regularly coaches the team and follows them up on their work. It can be a good idea to encourage people to strategically move into the district where the church plant will take place.

Combination method: You hire a person to train a team of volunteers who together with this person plants a new church. The team consists of ordinary people who have ordinary secular jobs to earn their livings, but who are commissioned by the church through prayer to become the core leadership group of the new church. The person hired as church planter is primarily responsible for training the team members.

M1-2-4-3 The church planter method
A person is hired to plant a church far away from the mother church without receiving assistance from the mother church. We can distinguish between two models for this method, both models requiring a specially equipped worker with a clear vision and a great capacity to work independently.

1. A church planter who is hired as a pioneer by the denomination: A worker with a family moves into a completely new area to start a church. The church planter is alone at the beginning and has to do all the work himself/herself.

2. A church planter who organizes one or more evangelism outreaches in an area without a church presence: This is more or less the same pattern as above, but the starting point here is to organize evangelism outreaches done by Christians who commit a week or two of their summer holidays to do this. During the outreach a number of people living in the area shows interest in the gospel, who the church planter contacts after the outreach for follow-up.

M1-2-4-4 Other methods
Some churches choose to cross heavy cultural barriers and work among certain hard-to-reach ethnic groups and sub-cultures in their society. Others target particular geographic or cultural groups: church members share the gospel with unsaved friends from these groups and build bridges into the culture as they go, with the hope of establishing a fellowship within the target group. This method is common in *missional* churches: Fellowships are started for specific groups of people, such as media people, politicians, artists and musicians, business and industry. It could also be student fellowships that emerge on campus. In

many places the church's presence is a mixture of various missional fellowships consisting of specific target groups that have been reached with the gospel.

In the church planting literature we use the terms *incarnational, missional, attractional* and *proclamational. Incarnational* means 'go out and stay there'. The term is often used in the church planting literature when a small group (5-10 people) enters a culture, establishes a church and then allows the church to take on various characteristics of that culture. *Missional* means 'go out and invite'. The planting strategy itself is defined by the target group you wish to reach, meaning that the main focus in the planting is directed towards one particular target group, such as students or young families, for example. *Attractional* means 'invite'. This term describes a planting strategy where you say "come to us." You create programs, activities, and church services that are attractive to your target group in order to reach out to them. We believe that church planting should consist of elements from all three of these models; but the strategy you choose for the first phase of your ministry will probably focus on just one of them. *Proclamational* is simply proclaiming the gospel with little emphasis on accompanying works of service.

We need to be flexible in form, expression, and the way we plant new fellowships. We've learned that it is important that church planters from different church denominations and organizations come together and learn from each other's models and methods. This has been going on in Norway for many years now.[125] In the past few years different learning networks have emerged among church planters and the fellowships they've planted. This has led to a higher rate of newly established fellowships.[126]

M1-2-4-5 Theological foundations

While church planters focus on choosing which model and method to use for their work, they also have to be deeply anchored in the Word of God and in the unchanging gospel. In our opinion it is important to reflect on your personal theological standpoint. We have to know where we stand theologically, while at the same time have an open mind to all of God's people who may or may not share our theological views. The kingdom of God is the focus, not us. It is his church, not ours. On a number of occasions I've been asked to consult church-planting teams made up of individuals from different church backgrounds and theological views. They've asked me what I think they should do. My answer to them has been: Agree at the beginning which theological foundation the new

[125] The Church Planting Network of Norway has gathered church planters and leaders to joint national conferences and forums in order to learn from each other, exchange experiences and challenge each other.

[126] Appleton, Joanne. *ECPN Concept Paper: Mid Sized Mission - The Use of Mid Sized Groups as a Vital Strategic Component of Church Planting.* Published on Leadnet.org, 2008.

[127] John 17:23

[128] Ephesians 3:17-18

church will be built on. Be honest with each other from the start, because it doesn't get easier to talk about theological issues as time goes on.

I feel God is doing something new across traditional church denominations and organizations. A new unity is arising that crosses over old borderlines. What they hold in common is an understanding that the kingdom of God is more then just the local church or the denomination we serve in. It is an acknowledgement that when they are brought to complete unity, "Then the world will know that you sent me and have loved them even as you have loved me."[127] So that we "being rooted and established in love, may have power, together with all the Lord's holy people, to grasp how wide and long and high and deep is the love of Christ."[128] New networks based on relationship are emerging in many places. They have a strong longing to seek God together and to see his intervention on our continent. There is a growing generosity in sharing resources with each other, to celebrate each other's victories and to bring comfort in defeat. I am convinced that God is doing this to prepare us for a time when the gospel will again advance on our continent. I meet a lot of young church planters who don't live in a traditional church context. They've seen God suddenly gather people to them. From being a gang of only four or five people they suddenly found themselves surrounded by 50-60 people—and more were getting saved. God is doing something new. At a time like this it is crucial that church planters and leaders listen to the Spirit of God and dare to do what he says.

M1-2-5   Commitment and accountability in relationships

M1-2-5-1   Long-term commitment

Starting a church requires a long-term commitment. Building up a thriving fellowship or a network of smaller groups can easily take from four to seven years. Commitment in the core team is one of the most important elements needed to succeed in church planting.

When I had the core team make a long-term commitment to our church planting work in Hånes it helped us to focus on building together. It gave us peace. Commitment is not just saying, "I'm in." It means investing in new friendships—and investing time and money as well. This is the kind of commitment Paul praises the church of Macedonia for:

"And they exceeded our expectations, they gave themselves first of all to the Lord, and then by the will of God also to us."[129]

[129] 2 Corinthians 8:5

This kind of commitment does not have one's own ego at the center, but the kingdom of God. It's about submitting to one another, about being open and honest in one's closest relationships. All of this is needed for a new fellowship to grow. The team members should hold each other accountable to their commitment. Ask each other: "How do you feel about committing to the work and starting a new church? How long are you willing to commit for? What are your spiritual gifts, and how can you contribute to making the vision we share come true?"

The early pioneer phase of a church-planting team is a wonderful time. It is characterized by excitement and joy, unity and a sense of being a family; it is filled with faith, optimism and energy, vision and group identity, with a willingness to give and to sacrifice. It is an organic phase filled with quick decisions and a strong "us-feeling." In this phase you will form the culture of the church that will be carried on to the next growth phase. It is important, therefore, that there is continuity in the core group. This phase will illuminate the leader's potential, and his or her faithfulness and willingness to serve is tested and revealed. It is not a given that the most gifted ones are the most faithful; character goes before charisma. Therefore you should be slow to assign people to permanent leadership positions in the earliest phase of church planting.

Commitment also deals with finances. Start giving to the community as early as possible. Our heart follows our money. How we manage our money in the core team sets the standard for how others will give to the church. The core team has to lead in generosity and in the joy of giving. As a church planter and leader you should trust the finances of the church to someone else, with an openness and transparency in these matters. A church planter must have the ability to rely on outside help when needed—especially when it comes to finances. There needs to be good communication about the flow of money on a church-planting ministry. Living in close and accountable relationships is important both for the core team and for the church planter. You have to understand what the Word of God teaches about being under authority and being in accountable relationships.

[130] Matthew 28:18

[131] Matthew 7:29

[132] John 4:34

[133] Hebrews 10:5-7

[134] John 5:19

M1-2-5-2 Standing under healthy authority

Jesus says, "All authority in heaven and on earth has been given to me."[130] Jesus has the final authority and power. He *was* and *is* almighty. The people who surrounded Jesus saw that he used his power and authority: "Because he taught as one who had authority, and not as their teachers of the law."[131] The authority of Jesus was given to him because he was under an authority himself.

> "My food" said Jesus, "is to do the will of him who sent me and to finish his work."[132]

The author of the letter to the Hebrews writes:

> Therefore, when Christ came into the world, he said: "Sacrifice and offering you did not desire, but a body you prepared for me; with burnt offerings and sin offerings you were not pleased. Then I said, 'Here I am – it is written about me in the scroll – I have come to do your will, my God'."[133]

> "Jesus gave them this answer: "Very truly I tell you, the Son can do nothing by himself; he can do only what he sees his Father doing, because whatever the Father does the Son also does."[134]

Jesus' power and authority lie in his obedience to his Father. What can we learn from this? You have no authority unless you stand under authority yourself. We often have negative associations toward the words *authority* and *power*. Jesus didn't. If we look at the book of Revelations we find a description of Jesus as "the Lamb of God" and "the Lion of Judah." They are apparently opposites but together they show us the core of his vision of power and authority in leadership. The Lamb stands for humbleness and sacrifice, purity and kindness. The Lion symbolizes lordship and conquest, justice and kingship. The author Romano Guardini says:

> "We are made in the image of God, and to show the whole image of him we must act in power and authority (rule) at the same time as we serve. To rule without serving leads to selfishness and abuse of power. Only through the unity of the two, when both elements come into their own, will man become whole and reach the completion of his calling." [135]

Guardini defines power as "the ability to make decisions."[136] We use our power through our decisions and lack of decisions. As followers of Jesus we learn how to make good decisions when we live under his lordship and willingly stand under his authority. Only those who stand under authority are able exercise power and authority in a good and healthy manner.

M1-2-5-3 Living in accountable relationships

Jesus is "the head of the body" and through him "we will grow to become in every respect the mature body of him who is the head."[137] But Jesus is not just 'head' but also 'body' -- he speaks through his body today, through Christian brothers and sisters. This is why it is extremely important for me as a church planter to be tightly knitted to others to whom I have given the authority to speak into my life – to encourage, help, counsel and correct me. The authors of this book want to emphasize the importance of being under authority. As church planters we all have someone we've given authority to help, coach, and correct us. We meet regularly with these people. We believe this is the key for all church planters in maintaining and developing a healthy authority as leaders of a new church. Do you have people around you like this? Who are they? In what ways do they give you guidance and support? Are you willing to listen to them? Many of the themes we've touched on here will emerge when you are building a healthy core team in the early stages of a new fellowship. Team building will be the subject of the next chapter.

[135] Guardini, Romano. *Das Ende der Neuzeit - Die Macht.* Mainz: Matthias-Grünewald Verlag, 4. oppl. 2001.

[136] Ibid. Guardini writes that Power (to make decisions) = energy + physical strength + the awareness that understands this power + a will and initiative to direct this power toward a goal + the ability to lead that power toward the goal. Power is thus the ability to make decisions.

[137] Ephesians 4:12 and 15

M1-3

[138] Genesis 1:26

[139] John 5:16-30

[140] Luke 10:1-2

[141] Ephesians 1:3-11;
4:11-13

[142] 1 Corinthians 12:13

BUILDING THE CORE TEAM – BY TERJE DAHLE

M1-3-1   Introduction

Working together as a team can be a fantastic thing—dynamic, and full of creativity and joy. But it can also be incredibly exhausting when heated debates and lack of direction overtake the team. Psalm 133 describes a team that is good to be on and that bears good fruit: "How good and pleasant it is when God's people live together in unity!"

Everyone who has experienced this knows that there is absolutely nothing else that can provide the same satisfaction and create the same long-lasting healthy results than living in unity with other believers on a church planting team. The Bible tells us that God has always worked together as the Trinity. God says: "let us make mankind in our image."[138] Jesus demonstrated the Trinitarian relationship in a number of ways: For example, he didn't do anything without the Father showing it to him first.[139] And when he sent the disciples out to preach the good new of the Kingdom, he sent them out two-by-two—never alone.[140]

When faced with God's greatness, glory, and power, we can get totally overwhelmed by the massive scale of his plans and purposes. The only thing we can do is humbly admit that our part in God's plan is way too big for us to do it alone.[141] God's greatness helps us to see that *diversity and unity* are two sides of the same coin: we need each other as co-workers to see God's kingdom established on Earth. Paul describes us as being "baptized by one Spirit so as to form one body."[142] The human body consists of millions of cells, but they work together in creating an amazing diversity of functions that cooperate to make us this fantastic organism. Being baptized with the Holy Spirit in the body of Christ means that the human dividing lines of language, culture, age, and sex cannot separate us any more as Christians. To be filled with the Spirit of God makes us co-laborers rather then individualists. The Holy Spirit shows us our common mission and how we need each other's strengths and skills to overcome the challenges we face together.

In the letters of Paul in the New Testament we find several images of the church that underline the unity we experience when we work together. "We are members of the body of Christ, built together to become a dwelling place, the family of God."[143]

In Ephesians Chapter 6, when Paul speaks of a warrior who stands and fights against evil, the term he uses has an individual and collective connotation. Breaking new ground, starting new churches and preaching the gospel is an individual responsibility and something we do together. One isn't done at the expense of the other. This biblical image shows us that we have both a personal and corporate responsibility as followers of Jesus Christ.

M1-3-2   Leaders in the Bible worked together on teams

On the day of Pentecost Peter came forward together with the Eleven.[144] From the beginning the apostles worked together as the leadership team for the church in Jerusalem. They are described as a group in several places in the Book of Acts.[145] "The elders" is a common term in the Bible for the leaders of a church. The expression has a history that goes back to the patriarchs in the Old Testament. When the apostles appointed leaders of a new church, they were appointed as *elders*.[146] "Elders" is a plural word. We can see an example of this when Paul calls for the leadership in Ephesus:[147] a group came to meet Paul – they came as a *team*.

Paul never worked alone in ministry. When he was going on his first mission trip[148] he was sent by the Holy Spirit to go together with Barnabas. In the Epistles we can see how Paul is always surrounded by his co-workers. In Acts 17 we clearly see how much it meant to Paul to work together with the others: Paul arrives alone in Athens because there was so much persecution and trouble on the island of Berea that they had to make him leave. Verse 16 tells us that: "While Paul *was waiting for them* in Athens, he was greatly distressed to see that the city was full of idols" – he was waiting for the arrival of Timothy and Silas. Even when circumstances caused Paul to work alone, he still preferred to work with his teammates.

M1-3-3   Teamwork as the answer to today's challenges

Many of the challenges the first Christians faced are the same we see in our society today.[149] This also affects the churches. *Pax Romana* was a famous term

[143] Ephesians 2:19-22; 4:15-16

[144] Acts 2:14

[145] Acts 4:33; 5:12; 8:12; 9:27

[146] Acts 14:23

[147] Acts 20:17-38

[148] Acts 13:1ff

[149] McNeal, Reggie. *Revolution in Leadership: Training Apostles for Tomorrow's Church.* Nashville, TN: Abingdon Press, 1999

[150] Acts 2:9-11

[151] Acts 17:16

[152] Ephesians 4:11-13

used in the Roman Empire. The Romans ruled the world, built roads for trading, providing peace and wealth to all those who surrendered to their lordship. The Christians got into trouble because they would only recognize Jesus Christ as their Lord. The Roman Empire experienced globalization,[150] pluralism (diversity of religions), spiritual awakening (a growing distance between established religion and folklore (Gnosticism)) and individualism.[151] Teamwork helps us when faced with the challenges of today that often hinder the progress of the kingdom of God. We can sort out difficult thought processes when we work together, such as:

Finding a balance between equipping people for service while discouraging a destructive hierarchical mindset that tends to make people passive.[152]

Continue to break new ground instead of stopping to maintain earlier work.

To think and process together as a team while avoiding an "us – them" or "layman – scholar" attitude.

To think holistically without making an artificial distinction between spiritual and secular matters.

M1-3-4 Foundational reasons for the individual to work in a team situation

M1-3-4-1 The individual and the whole

It is the sum of the individual members that determines whether or not a team becomes a dynamic ministry that breaks new ground. Some skills can be taught along the way by working together. But there are certain basic elements that function as foundational building blocks for creating a dynamic team. If we ignore these we might be up for a surprise.

When I started leading the prayer group that eventually ended up being a church, I learned how quickly I started to compare myself with others. I often found that others were better than me in many ways. I wasn't musical, organized, or good at communication, teaching or preaching when I viewed myself in the light of other's talents. It made me passive and a bystander more than a participant in many occasions. When I later had an encounter with the unconditional love of God and started to understand what it means to be a new creation in Christ Jesus, a new kind of security came into my life. It made me relax a lot more when I met other people. I could look at people as my co-workers and not as my competitors. I got more involved, took initiative, and rejoiced in the dynamics that begin when everybody shares their hearts. From that time on teamwork has been one of my favorite parts of serving in the kingdom of God.

M1-3-4-2 Three basic factors for successful teamwork:

(I) The Grace of God. The grace of God creates an identity based on the work of God and not our own.[153] This frees us from conditional love, competition and comparison. We let the gospel become flesh and blood through us so that we are characterized by a trust in God[154] and the experience of being a new creature.[155]

(II) Confident in your own identity. Confident people recognize the importance of others.[156] Instead of looking at other people's gifts and talents as a threat, confident people who understand the grace of God embrace and appreciate other people's calling and equipping. You then relate to other people without having a hierarchical mindset built upon positions and titles. You have different values; you place Jesus and the plan of God in the center. We all become his servants and equally important on a common mission.

(III) Revelation of the body of Jesus Christ. We see the church as a body[157] with Jesus Christ as the head.[158] With a holistic perspective like this we get the right picture of others and ourselves. We become members of Christ himself and get the right kind of self-respect based on being important to the whole. People are appreciated because they each represent different talents and contribute to make the whole of the body of Jesus Christ real. This will put an end to our comparison and false inferiority.[159] We also put an end to operating independently of others.[160] The body works as a unit, showing care and concern for each member. No one does anything at the expense of someone else, because we are governed by Christ as the head and he shows no favoritism.[161]

M1-3-5 Shared values and vision – the foundation for successful teamwork

M1-3-5-1 The anchoring of vision and values

A successful team ministry is founded on shared vision and values. All of this can be linked to how we perceive God and how this affects us. The way we view God affects the way we view the world, our self-esteem, and what we see as our purpose in life. Thus our vision and values should be anchored in the God of

[153] Ephesians 2:4-10

[154] Romans 8:5-17

[155] 2 Corinthians 5:17

[156] Matthew 22:36-40

[157] 1 Corinthians 12

[158] Ephesians 1:22-23; 4:15

[159] 1 Corinthians 12:14-18

[160] 1 Corinthians 12:20-26

[161] Galatians 2:6; Romans 2:11

162 1 John 4:17 the Bible, who is outside of us, so that they have substance when faced with the realities of church planting.

When Lise and I moved to Vesterålen in northern Norway in 1984, we saw many young people get saved. Our house was filled with people who were hungry to see more of God. At that time we didn't have any real thoughts about starting up a church, or a sense of calling that we were to lead. But we did feel responsible for the people who got saved, so we began to regularly gather in fellowship with those who received the gospel. Other Christians joined us because they wanted to take part in what was happening. After some time we addressed the subject of vision and values with the group, and it soon became clear that there were a lot of different opinions among those who had joined the work. The process of clarifying a vision and values actually made several leave the fellowship. Just by saying that we wanted to build a church and not just stay a prayer group made someone leave. For those people who stayed on, this difficult process created a shared focus on the ministry and a desire to live together as a church. It gave us a sense of peace in the ministry and we avoided continuous tensions within the church.

M1-3-5-2 Shared values

Values are those things that mean something to us, things that we're willing to fight for. For us, values originate in God.[162] They guide us when we face challenges and they give parameters for the way we do our work. All the members in our team are aware of our team values and know how to relate to them. We live in integrity. We model a culture where people are true to their word and to their obligations, and we respect each other's things, such as time. We use the same measure on ourselves as we do with others and the decisions we make are founded on our values. We avoid shortcuts to reach short-term goals. When mercy is one of our core values we don't see people for what they can offer, but we show mercy without thinking of getting anything in return.

It is important that values are not taken for granted, but are communicated to people in such a way that they are conscious of them and make them part of their lives. Values will then serve as the glue that holds the fellowship together and create a shared identity. Identity should not come from leaders or gifts but through something deep and God-given. Values also generate standards on how we live together: what we say to whom, what kind of humor we have and so on. Being conscious of our values prevents a culture from falling apart. Unspoken norms give growth to misunderstandings and can make us jump to conclusions. Values should be written so clearly that they set the patterns you want your ministry to be characterized by. Examples of such patterns can be:

» We talk with each other, not about each other.

» We never try to cover our tracks.

» We speak our minds no matter what we think others might think of it.

M1-3-5-3 Shared vision

When we have a personal encounter with the grace of God, we enter into a corporate call and vision shared by the body of Christ.[163] We see that the goal we share with others on the church planting team is more important than whatever role or function we have on the team. We don't become threatened by others, but do what we need to reach our common goal. This makes us flexible and creates within us an ability to adapt that makes it easier for everyone to work together. A "me-focus" destroys many teams by allowing our personal convictions get in the way of the whole. A personal agenda can become a sidetrack that steals energy and attention that can wear out a church-planting team in the long run. Planting a church demands that focus and energy is unified in a common direction. A unified vision creates space in a unified direction that allows for different types of people with different gifts and abilities to participate on the team.

A shared vision in the kingdom of God is much more than just gathering people together to share thoughts and ideas about the future. It is to embody the revelation God has given us of Jesus Christ in flesh and blood. It has its origins in the heavenly realms and has a foundation that can endure the tests and pressures that come with a pioneering work.[164]

M1-3-5-4 The interdependence of team members

As Paul describes it, we are one body in which all its members are necessary for its working, requiring that all function with respect and care for all others. This assumes a mutual respect and care for each other.[165] Our significance is not determined by our skills and gifts but by the fact that through his mercy we are included in the body of Christ. This is anchored outside of us. The team is as strong as its weakest link. It is therefore important that the team has someone who is capable of seeing the team as a whole, so that important functions are

[163] Hebrews 3:1

[164] Matthew 16:15-18

[165] 1 Corinthians 12:21-26

[166] 2 Corinthians 8:5

[167] Genesis 1:28

not overlooked. The apostolic aspect of pioneering is to see the whole in relation to the prophetic and evangelistic functions. When the team members are interdependent with each other, it means that each person must have a clear commitment to God and to each other.[166] Interdependence must be defined on the team as to how this works out practically within the team's daily routines. The practical outworking of interdependence includes:

Working through conflicts without pushing them away or ignoring them;

Knowing what each person's responsibilities on the team are;

A mutual expectation that each person gives their all for the ministry, respecting each person's unique capacity and energy levels;

While the team must be willing to take chances, there must be enough security on the team that even those who tend to take things more cautiously will dare to do things in a new or different way.

M1-3-5-5 Understand each other's significance

When you have a holistic vision of the interdependence of each team member, you are able to see the *significance* of each person's unique call and skill set within the context of the entire team. You avoid conflicts caused by people thinking that others are standing in the way of their own call being realized. You also avoid people being inhibited from stepping out in ministry because they don't see how their gifts can be used on the team. A revelation of the power of the Cross will help each team member converge at a common focal point, who is Jesus Christ. In Jesus there is room for everyone— each person fulfilling an indispensable role in presenting to the world the body of Christ in all its amazing color and diversity. The kingdom of God advances when each of God's people does what he or she is uniquely equipped and called to do, working in sync with each other's functions and gifts. If not – kingdom advancement can be seriously hindered by the frustration and confusion caused by a lack of appreciation for the significance each of member.

M1-3-5-6 Reproduction and multiplication

When we function as one body we create the conditions for the body to reproduce itself. God imbedded this in our very nature, calling us to be fruitful and multiply.[167] Jesus demonstrated this in his ministry by investing time in the lives of the disciples before relinquishing his earthly ministry to them. Paul teaches this to Timothy, admonishing him to live in the same manner he does.[168] We can also read about four generations of Christians that served God together. [169]

When we are pioneering a new work, it is tempting to evaluate progress by looking at numbers and figures – they're easy to measure and to communicate to others. But if we model God's way of doing ministry, we will invest in a select few individuals, which actually *increases* the potential for growth. We don't spend time with these people just so that they can do our work for us and serve us! We invest in their lives in order to help them find their place in the body of Christ so that they can function at their optimal level. Through this we release people into ministry, where they grow into mature laborers. We sow and water these individuals, but it is God who gives the increase by releasing his life into them.[170] This is the only form of ministry that gives both quantitative and qualitative growth. It has a long-term perspective that unites several generations of workers together. As we work as the body of Christ, we need each other to get the job done—but this doesn't mean that we (mis)use each other in a negative way. When we think in terms of reproduction, we structure our team in a way that those who have some level of responsibility find someone to invest in who will take over that area of responsibility in the future. This encourages reproduction in all functions and tasks on the team.

This kind of long-term planning and investment is crucial for producing sustainable growth in a pioneer church-planting situation. You avoid the "boomerang effect" of ministry growth, which comes back and hits you in the head because you hadn't increased your team's capacity for growth ahead of time. It also reduces the potential for team burnout while preserving core team values such as family life, recreation and rest.

M1-3-5-7 Team communication

The foundation for successful teamwork is good communication.[171] Good communication is dependent on a learning-based culture characterized by openness and focus on the ministry. The ideal is for information to flow freely through the whole team so that the time team members spend together can be used to discuss the things that are currently going on. Victories are celebrated and defeats can be discussed openly. In this way you develop a culture and a "language" of communication that will form the basis for a good flow of

[168] 2 Timothy 2:1-2

[169] Matthew 28:18-20;
John 20:21

[170] 1 Corinthians 3:6

[171] Maxwell, John. *The 17 Indisputable Laws of Teamwork.* Thomas Nelson, 2001.

[172] Acts 1:14

[173] Acts 13:1-3

[174] 1 Timothy 2:1-4; Acts 4:23-24

[175] Luke 18:1-5

information and a shared identity within the group. A certain look or an inside comment can be all it takes to make everybody laugh or nod in recognition.

M1-3-5-8 Openness in communication

Jesus has called *all* of us to discipleship, which means that *none* of us are perfect. This forms the foundation for openness and nearness in team communication. Jesus walked together with the disciples in their daily lives and shared with them with immediacy and directness. If communication is characterized by argumentation, it hinders the flow of good conversation and ideas. Openness starts with the team leader. It is important to share more than just the ministry with each other: openness comes to life by sharing from our own lives. "How are things going with our families?" "How's it going with your health, personal prayer life, your financial situation?" When we start with our own lives and share openly with the others we build a bridge of nearness and trust.

Openness is based on praying and seeking God together.[172] Spending time together in prayer nurtures a spiritual unity on the team that affects the way we communicate with each other. Planting a new church is a spiritual endeavor that is based on the interconnection of *vertical communication* (talking with God) and *horizontal communication* (sharing as a team).[173]

The driving force of team ministry is collectively calling on the name of God and sharing the experience of hearing God together.[174] This takes endurance, something that Jesus was fully aware of.[175] Praying together strengthens us and helps us stay focused on prayer that is so important when we go through challenging times.

M1-3-5-9 Good communication has the following characteristics:

Mutual commitment. Everyone is there for each another, and we feel that we can trust each other. We talk *with* each other, not *about* each other. We never say things about each other in inappropriate settings, and what has been said in confidence stays that way.

Teachability. We listen to each other to learn, increase our understanding and gain new insight and knowledge. We don't come to our times together with a fighting spirit but with an inquisitive attitude.

No fear. When we share with each other, we give frequent and prompt responses to avoid creating communication vacuums and insecurity. Responses should be clear and unambiguous to steer clear of confusion and the need to speculate as to what the other means.

No surprises. Communication needs to flow to each member who needs to receive it. This ensures that no one feels left out or that they are missing important information. There shouldn't be any private discussions carried or agreements made outside of the appropriate forums.

Trust. Communication needs to be honest— even when it costs and is uncomfortable for both sender and receiver. There are no hidden agendas in what is said or not said.

Speaking in faith and accountability. We speak with an "I-message" when we have something on our hearts to share, and steer clear of using others to promote our own view. We should never speak on behalf of others. We stand by what we say and we are responsible for all the things we say or do not say. Everyone is clear on what they mean, daring to be personal in their approach to each other so that it is easy to relate to one another.

M1-3-5-10 Openness to change

Teams are not static or unchangeable. Our position on the team isn't above our function or task. The team should consist of those who at any given time are best equipped to complete the task. A personal openness to change keeps the ministry flexible, and guards us from shifting focus away from team goals and onto some personal agenda in relation to our own place and function on the team. A healthy team embraces and adapts to change—even living in and expecting change (cf. Acts 13:1-3). Self-reflection helps us to see ourselves and our function realistically in light of the whole. We must dare to have the uncomfortable conversations that lead to change in roles and functions on the team.

M1-3-5-11 Cooperation and teachability

Paul utilized his co-workers by sending them out on various trips to visit the churches. The work was not characterized by "mine" and "yours" but by "ours." Seeing your work in the same way—with a common purpose and call based on a flat organizational structure—helps you to cooperate with a wide variety of people, avoiding the pitfalls of competition and comparison. Being in open dialogue with team members during a decision-making process places your decision on a broad foundation of experience and insight. Cooperation based on shared values promotes a culture of learning that opens the team to continuous development. You can encourage team members to read and learn new things, and then to share what they've learned with the others. In planning processes where issues are discussed over a longer period of time, it is important not to jump to quick conclusions that stop the process too early. Avoid having the team leader speak his mind first during a discussion: this is a great way to short-circuit any further input from the rest of the team.

M1-3-5-12 Conflicts in communication

Conflicts go hand-in-hand with teamwork. The reasons for this can be divided into different areas:

» Different values

» Different visions

» Different role expectations

» Different perceptions of reality

It is important to discover the underlying issues that lead to a conflict. If it is based on conflicting vision and/or values, it can be very difficult to solve the conflict without changing the composition of the team. It is important not to avoid the uncomfortable questions, but to face them openly and honestly. Support and supervision from outside the team is often necessary to solve a conflict. The relationships you need for this kind of assistance should be built during good times so that you have conflict-resolution resources in place *before* a conflict arises. But if these resources are merely based on structure – that a person is sent from the mother church without having any real relationship or trust built with the church-planting team in crisis, for example – this type of help is quite often of little use in resolving a team conflict.

Conflicts must be resolved. Unresolved, persistent conflict robs the team of its energy and focus and can ultimately lead to the breakdown of the team. You can't just leave things and hope for the best; you have to talk about things, address areas of conflict, identify challenges, and then make a concrete plan that will help you move forward.

M1-3-5-13 Building personal character through team ministry

A good ministry team is created when people's character and gifts match the tasks they do. There is no replacement for the fruit of the Spirit.[176] Walking in the Spirit involves not being driven by vain ambition, but working together towards a common goal.

A sense of personal responsibility and commitment is essential when the team comes under pressure and faces resistance. When a team has stood together in the midst of trials, the team members develop a deep sense of belonging and commitment to each other that prepares them for the challenges awaiting them in the next church-planting phase. This cohesiveness becomes evident when the team pulls together to get a job done—even when the job isn't exactly someone's favorite thing to do.

A team situation builds character in us when the others grate on us and get under our skin – to touch us in areas of our lives that we would rather keep hidden.[177] Not dodging tensions but facing them and working through them builds character in us. And it also gives us experiences that open our eyes to see teamwork as a good way of doing ministry. One of the best compliments we can receive is when someone tells you that they can count on you—knowing that you can count on them and the rest of the team as well.

M1-3-5-14 The fruit of team ministry

A well-functioning ministry team brings results on many levels; it is also visionary, outward-focused and empowering. It endures the test of time and reproduces gifts and functions in others. It supports new ways of thinking that releases initiative. And one more thing: It's fun!

[176] Galatians 5:22-26

[177] Proverbs 27:17

M 1 - 4

CLEAR VISION – BY ØYSTEIN GJERME

[178] Isaiah 6:1-7

[179] Isaiah 6:8

[180] Nehemiah 2:1-6

M1-4-1   Introduction

God's plan of salvation advances when he handpicks people and calls them to carry out particular assignments for him. The experience of receiving a call is unique and subjective, and those who hear a call can choose not to respond to it. But when a call is responded to, acted upon and met with certain circumstances in a particular historical context, it can have major significance for God's activity in the world. The stories of how people in the Bible experienced their call and what they did in response to that call, give us an idea about how visions are formed. We will take a look at five examples below.

M1-4-2   Experiences of receiving a call in the Bible

M1-4-2-1   Isaiah – encounter with God

Isaiah's call started when he saw God, and experienced how his sense of guilt was removed from him. Through this experience he was put in right relationship with God.[178] When God then asked him "Whom shall I send? And who will go for us?" he answered, "Here am I. Send me!"[179] It was his encounter with God that led him to the particular need he was called to meet.

M1-4-2-2   Nehemiah – a social need that led to an encounter with God

Nehemiah worked in the palace of the king of Persia in Babylon. He was one of the descendants of the Jews who had been exiled to Persia. One day he received word about how terrible the conditions were for those who had returned to Jerusalem. He cried and prayed for many days and asked God for an opportunity to return and rebuild the wall around Jerusalem.[180] This is a wonderful story of how a specific need in society made someone seek God. Nehemiah was granted permission to lead a group of Jews back to Jerusalem, who had great success in rebuilding the wall—in just 52 days. Later he received a call from God to lead the Jewish people into a renewed understanding of God's will for their lives.

M1-4-2-3   Moses – surprised by God

Moses had a surprising encounter with God. He was far removed from his previous life when God met him in a burning bush. God said:

"Do not come any closer, take off your sandals, for the place where you are standing is holy ground." Then he said, "I am the God of your father, the God of Abraham, the God of Isaac and the God of Jacob." At this Moses hid his face, because he was afraid to look at God.[181]

[181] Exodus 3:5-6

[182] Exodus 3:10-11

[183] Numbers 13 and 14

For Moses, this encounter with God was also an encounter with himself. After receiving the call: "I am sending you to Pharaoh to bring my people the Israelites out of Egypt", he was able to put into words how he felt about himself by saying, "Who am I?"[182]

M1-4-2-4   Joshua – faithful against the stream

Joshua was one of the scouts Moses had sent to explore the promised land of Canaan. After the scouts returned the majority of the Israelites where terrified of what to expect of their opponent. But Joshua was one in the minority who chose to believe God. Through the situation he caught the vision: The Israelites had wandered many years in the desert; now the time had come to enter the land that God had promised them and that Moses had led them to.[183]

M1-4-2-5   Paul – an encounter with Jesus

Saul became Paul after he had his life changed by an encounter with Jesus. He was a resistor of the followers of Jesus from Nazareth and he was on his way to Damascus to persecute them. On his way he was thrown to the ground and confronted by the one he was persecuting— Jesus himself. Paul's theological and practical guidance made him one of the most influential persons when the early church movement was formed. Everything that he wrote, did, and preached can be traced back to his experience on the road to Damascus—his encounter with Jesus.

These five call experiences have three things in common. First, they all describe a respect for, and an encounter with, God. Second, they express the sense that God has an agenda that they can be of service to. And third, the assignments are so concrete that they are able to grasp it within their own situations.

[184] Habakkuk 2:2

[185] Malphurs, Aubrey. *Values-Driven Leadership*. Grand Rapids: Baker, 1996 (p174).

[186] Our vision for life is to lead people to a better life by following Jesus. Our vision for the church is to build a strong a continuously growing local church that keeps on expanding to new networks and areas through multiplication of our call, culture and church community. Our greater vision is to be a center for innovation, equipping and training so that people can find and fill the place God has reserved for them and by this assists the kingdom of God to expand locally, nationally and globally.

[187] Wilson, Scott. *2000: Challenge of Leadership. What Leaders Do Next*. Denmark: Royal 2000 (pp 33-43).

M1-4-3 Why is a clear vision so important?

M1-4-3-1 A written vision gives information and freedom

A clearly articulated vision is crucial, especially in the early stages of the church-planting effort. The vision serves as an invitation for others to come join the work, and gives a simplified answer to the question "Which challenge should we solve?" Clarifying the vision will help people find out whether they want to help and to what extent they want to get involved.

When God called the prophet Habakkuk he said, "Write down the revelation and make it plain on tablets so that whoever reads it may run with it!"[184] In other words, it should be easy and understandable to people so that it releases energy for what lies ahead. The challenge is to write the vision in a way that it is easily applicable to people's daily lives. When I was formulating the vision for our church-planting ministry I read through the vision and values statements of many different churches; I could easily see that most of them had a "collective language."[185] There was very little space given to *me,* "the individual"; and, in light of the analysis of current social trends, we considered it wise to answer the question "What am *I* supposed to do?" Thus we structured the vision statement for our church with three separate parts: a life vision, a church vision and a greater vision.[186] We wanted to meet people in their daily lives through the first part, create a sense of institutional belonging with the second and make room for future expansion in the third.

A written vision should have a long-term perspective. In the Salt Bergen Church we used the Procedural-model developed by Dr. Scott Wilson to give direction to our vision. In contains three important elements, where the vision or *promise* is the first element. The second element, which is retrieved from the key words found in the vision, is the church's *values*. These values determine the culture that will characterize the church and how it will reach its goals. The third element is the *process*, which is a clear articulation of how people and resources should be concretely prioritized to fulfill the vision.[187] It can be explained in more detail like this:

VISION: A statement consisting of three or four sentences that sets the direction by the leader(s) for a group of people. Lasts 20 to 30 years. Fletcher: "a prophetic image of God's preferred future."

VALUES: One-sentence statements based on key words taken directly from the vision statement that give moral and ethical clarity to the vision.

GOAL: A specific, measurable, and attainable statement expressed in terms of time, stating when something is to be completed. A goal should be expressed in terms of both quality and quantity.

STRATEGIES: Steps and methods that are developed in order to reach an overall goal.

» *Vision and values* belong to the leadership and are spiritual, easily understandable, and permanent.

» *Goals and strategies* belong to the people. They are technocratic and methodological and can be replaced from year to year.

» Most churches already have a special focus that can be made clear to all through a written vision.

» *Identity and purpose:* A clear vision makes it easier for people to find a church they can commit themselves to.

[188] An updated vision manual is published each year at the beginning of August.

This model for organizational management has served us well on the leadership level. With a set vision and established values we have been able to form a 'vision manual' that contains a description of what we directly work with. In the yearly update of the vision, a large number of ministry leaders are involved in shaping the goals and strategies to ensure that our efforts lead us in the same direction.[188]

M1-4-3-2 A written vision helps people to commit

The Norwegian volunteer culture has gone through a lot of changes the last years. These changes also affect the culture of volunteer work within church life. We experience that a clear vision makes it easier for people to consider what we are inviting them to commit to. A clear "yes" can also help people to say a clear "no" when they in fact don't wish to participate.

[189] Genesis 37

[190] Genesis 37:45

[191] Genesis 15:5-6

M1-4-3-3   A written vision clarifies a desired vision of the future

To start with the end in mind is a wise strategy. Very few church planters know what the vision of the future looks like in its entirety, but it is still wise to clarify what you see. The blurry parts can be described in a way that makes people curious, see possibilities, and want to join in. Robert Greenleaf says: "Not much happens without a dream. And for something great to happen, there must be a great dream. Behind every great achievement is a dreamer of great dreams."

A good example of this is the story about the dreamer Joseph. Just as Joseph's dreams evoked strong reactions from his brothers and family, our dreams can awaken reactions and resistance from people around us. This is because a dream is a vision of the future; it doesn't belong to the present. Joseph shared his dreams with his brothers and family like it was the most natural thing for him to do, and this provoked violent reactions.[189] In the story the dreams were born of God and meant to become real, but a fight broke out over of the very dream that ultimately turned out to be lifesaving for the people of Israel.[190]

To live a dream from God has a sharpness to it that separates one's companions from one's opponents. It is thus wise to articulate the dream clearly enough so people can easily pick their side.

People have many different motives for participating on a church-planting team. Many people throw themselves into new church-planting projects because they're afraid of missing out on something; others join because their friends and family have joined; still others do research *before* they join, in order to find out what it would mean to make a commitment to the ministry. It is very demanding to have people around you that you invest loads of time and energy in, but who are not moving toward the same vision of the future. Even though they contribute with enthusiasm and excitement for a while, it is only a matter of time before you will have to part ways. It can be painful for both those leaving and for those who remain. This is why it is an absolutely essential (and liberating) practice to make the end visible from the beginning!

M1-4-3-4   A written vision gives constant motivation and inspiration

A dream gives power on the way toward the goal. Abram, in his desperation and lack of a son complained to God; he was then told to go outside and count the stars. The result of this impossible task was that Abram believed God.[191] A dream that reveals the final goal gives constant motivation and inspiration along the way, because this kind of dream is woven together by a person's call, faith, and heart language. A leader should be able to communicate a vision so that it becomes a source of motivation and inspiration to others. We'll discuss later how this can be done.

[192] See Titus 2

M1-4-3-5 A vision makes people make a choice

The purpose of a vision is to gather a team of workers to make the stated goal come to life. It is an essential criterion that those who choose to join the journey must implicitly trust the leader's *motives,* the *method* to be used, and the *model* that will be followed.

First of all, it is important that workers trust the motives of the person or persons leading the work. Christian leadership is demanding. There are big expectations placed on the suitability of those who shoulder this kind of responsibility. On top of the outward evaluation of a leader's skills and standard of life, come all the various opinions people have regarding the motives the person has for leading the work.[192] How the motives of the leader are interpreted is greatly affected by the culture the church is being planted in. Cultures that are career-oriented can view a leader as someone who wants to realize him- or herself through a church-planting project. In hierarchically oriented cultures the leader can be perceived as someone who seeks power and influence. In the end it is necessary that the leader is given the opportunity to reveal his or her motives through the work of leading, which will validate the integrity of the person's motives.

Second, it is important that workers have faith in the *method* chosen to build the church. There are many different methods that can be used, though they all generally reflect the core values of Christian discipleship. The method is an expression of the ministry's "work form" and it is essential that this be made clear in order to gather people to the team who hold similar priorities. People can easily agree on where they want to go, but disagree on how to get there.

The third element you have to agree on is the *model* chosen to build the church plant after. There are many different church expressions and models that work, but it is essential that the fellowship agree to use the same "recipe". Making a clear distinction between business meetings, house churches, seeker-friendly churches, group-based churches and so on will help people understand the variation and power of making a choice. In the choice-based societies of the western world, there has emerged a marketplace for church models that people can orientate themselves by. The danger in this model-market is precisely that it is a *market*—a market that causes Christians to become model-shoppers.

My experience is that consumer-oriented behavior patterns lead to unfruitful attitudes and opinions that may ultimately lead people to become passive toward church life. Too many options can result in losing the whole concept of church. The church is not made to exist according to the premises of the market, and will therefore suffer under such circumstances.

M1-4-3-6 A vision makes people accountable to a direction and vision of the future

A clearly written vision is like a work description that is valid under any circumstances. It gives the church a deep keel in rough waters and high sails in times when you have a lot of energy. And so it is important to make sure that as many people as possible in the core group gain a sense of ownership for the vision. This is important for several reasons:

First of all, *mission drift* is a real danger for all organizations. This term refers to the unconscious process that leads an organization away from its original task. When faced with challenges and opportunities, it is easy to find short-term solutions while losing sight of the long-term goal. This kind of example becomes extremely obvious in mission work, where access to financial capital is great within missionary organizations involved in humanitarian work. At first glance this may look like a great opportunity to increase the effectiveness of the humanitarian side of the missions work. But this can often result in deprioritizing the original goal. In a church-planting ministry, a change in the age group, a change in demographics in the local area, or various team conflicts may lead one away from the original church-planting vision.

Second, it can be tempting for leaders who experience trouble in reaching their goal to "move the target" instead of staying accountable to the vision that lies as the foundation of the work. The visual and written vision is an easy tool to correct a bad course, holding both the leader and church responsible for their choices, priorities, and achievements.

Third, if you appoint a new main leader there is a real chance that the vision will change with him. Thus it is beneficial for the vision to have the broadest possible foundation within the core group so a potentially new leader recruited for the new church can work according to the original vision. There are various cultures within different traditions in this area, as well as different factors of the leadership style that is decisive for the outcome. In a phase when a vision is being changed or altered, there is a real danger that team members who began under the old vision will feel alienated from the new vision. It is therefore important to keep the vision as a guideline and a picture of the future. There are situations where a deliberate change is necessary but in these situations it is important that the vision be changed first before working on changing the character of the ministry.

[193] Ski, Martin. *Fram til Urkristendommen, Pinsevekkelsen gjennom 50 år.* Oslo: Filadelfiaforlaget, 1957 (p.134).

M1-4-4 How to create ownership of the vision

M1-4-4-1 Shared mission – local vision

The Great Commission applies to all Christians – but the vision for how the Great Commission should be accomplished must be *localized*. Every church-planting ministry should have a formulation for their vision that awakens passion in the hearts of the team members. A good vision is heartfelt, full of passion, and compelling. And, in contrast to most clubs, companies, and organizations there is also a criteria that the vision must have a deep foundation in the Christian faith. A good vision of the church is connected to the mission God has for the world: *Missio Dei.*

A local vision should answer the question "what problem are we going to work on?" The vision of the Salt Bergen Church is a result of our passion to be a church for the people of today. We wanted to set our spirituality free from the normal denominational lifestyle; so our discussions were based on questions like "what kind of church would *we* want to become members of?" "What do we need to do as Christians to make a difference in modern Norway?" "What does a normal week, month, and year look like in this kind of church?" "What do we have to do to make people see us as being *in* the world but not *of* it?" These questions and others have helped us to weave our church life together with our daily lives, releasing an ownership in our hearts for the church's vision.

M1-4-4-2 Deep roots and theological foundations

To establish a good foundation for our church planting ministry, the Salt Bergen Church has looked to the four pillars of the early church highlighted in Acts 2:42-47 – holding to the Word, fellowship, the breaking of the bread and to prayer. These keep us "looking toward the early church" and stay "in good company with the Pentecostal tradition."[193] But we've added a fifth pillar, so that the formulation of our church vision goes like this: *The Word, together, mission, close contact and change.* By highlighting these core practices we establish a

[194] Tangen, Karl Inge. *Ecclesial identification beyond transactional individualism? A case study of life strategies in growing late modern churches.* PhD thesis, Oslo, MF Norwegian School of Theology 2009 (p 226).

[195] Hirsch, Alan. *The Forgotten Ways.* Grand Rapids: Brazos, 2006 (p 24-25).

[196] Hirsh, p 26

point of contact between the priorities of the early church and motivating our own church to practice these in daily life.

Karl Inge Tangen has presented a model for postmodern churches that highlights the effect of emphasizing core practices.[194] The model emphasizes four fundamental *practice dynamics* each individual must figure out how to relate to: 1) the *narrative vision* with focus on the Word; 2) the *practice dynamic* with focus on the mission; 3) *participation in relationships* with focus on fellowship; and 4) *spirituality*, with focus on openness to the spiritual dimension. In the center of all these we find the postmodern individualist, who makes his or her own choices in relation to personal involvement in the church. In other words, the degree of one's participation is a question of *self-leading*. It is exactly this self-leading that determines the individual's awareness of the question: As a Christian, how and why do I make my choices?

In his book *The Forgotten Ways* Alan Hirch presents the term "Apostolic Genius": a systematic connection between the many factors that creates a growth movement.[195] He explores it throughout the book, but places all the various factors in one center with the headline "Jesus is Lord."[196] The level of involvement a postmodern individualist will have in church life and growth movements, according to Hirch, is solely dependent on the degree to which they lead themselves in line with the lordship of Jesus.

M1-4-4-3 Healthy focus
A vision must be relevant so that it is deemed trustworthy to those who are challenged to give themselves to it. Christian churches have developed their own genre of vision formulation; it is sad to see so many who write down statements of faith which in themselves are legitimate, but which lack any power to motivate. People are interested in knowing how a vision will make a difference in their lives, in their local area, and in their experience in participating in the Great Commission.

M1-4-4-4 Creating faith
People who commit themselves to a vision must feel sure that "if we do this we will change our world." In western, choice-based societies it is easy to get lost in the enormous selection of offers and alternatives. Because of this, a vision has to convey a sense of assurance that Christian discipleship will have an influence on the world. Over time, a vision's direction will help people to live it out in their

lives, which in turn helps to make the vision real. Ralph Emerson is the author behind the famous quote: "Do the thing, and you shall have the power." Nike simplified it to "Just do it", but the idea is still there: if you 'do it', you are headed in the right direction.

M1-4-4-5 Systematic vision management

Vision management is a responsibility that lies with the leadership. A wise way to approach this is by having an awareness of how the vision is kept alive in the different spheres of influential in the church. It should first be owned by the core leadership team, followed by the church members, and then be attractive to people outside the church.

The core of the church is the leadership team. These leaders are working with different time perspectives in their planning work, constantly measuring whether or not they are in line with the church vision. As mentioned earlier, the Church of Bergen formed a vision manual to explain how every department and area of ministry work together toward a common goal. We explain such things as our views on church services, our team-based church culture, and missions. The annual revisions we make in cooperation with the respective leaders ensure regular vision updates, course adjustments and adhesion to our core values. Everyone is challenged to think four years in advance and plan the next four quarters of the year in detail. In this way we ensure that even leaders who wouldn't describe themselves as visionary have the chance to catch a glimpse of what's in store for them.

The church consists of many different people who are involved in varying degrees. Christen leaders can easily be too concerned with their own perspective and underestimate the differences between their own views and the reality of people's daily life. Our experience shows us that a vision should be communicated through a number of different channels to ensure that the message is kept alive and well in the church.

Preaching is an important channel to communicate the vision to the church. It varies how far ahead different preachers plan their teaching, but it is clearly beneficial to be aware of how preaching can be used to underline the church's choices, values and profile, which together clarify the vision. But it is also important to work creatively to prevent repetitions that make listeners think that they've heard it all before, leading to indifference to the vision. One has to work hard to find new words, illustrations, and stories to create new approaches in sharing the vision.

Church media resources are also useful in communicating the vision. Before each service at the Church of Bergen, we run a film on the big screen that presents our vision and purpose. On the teachings we put out on podcasts, Mp3 and CDs, we begin by stating who we are and our purposes for being a church. We've also learned that an attractive webpage is useful for giving out important information.

The best and clearest way to communicate a vision is through good example. Illustrate what you want to achieve by having people share how they live, using them as examples of good decision-making and prioritizing. For example, if you want to build a church culture based on relationship, have people open up their homes, invite people into their lives, and showing hospitality. Church values of investing our time, resources, and service in the lives of others is best exemplified by people who actually *do* these things—acting as good role models for others. Stories and personal testimonies like these give a kick-start in pushing the church in the direction of the vision. But to make this happen you have to have a 'feedback culture' in the church so that these stories can be discovered. We've done this by encouraging people to share their stories in LIFE-groups and with others in the church.

Finally, it is important to make sure the vision is accessible to those who are on the outer-edges of the church's influence: those who only observe the church from the outside, those who haven't necessarily considered whether or not they're interested. What language do you use to share your vision with them? How do you communicate your vision visually? What other communication channels can you use? How do you present the church when dealing with the media? Put together, these can help create a reputation for the church that breaks down barriers and prejudices that others might have of the church.

M1-4-5   How to develop the vision

During the planning stages of the Church of Bergen, I was given a lot of freedom from the other leaders to work on a vision for the church. Having a vision is the prevailing practice in our church tradition, and I'm thankful that I was given the freedom to do this. This wasn't a difficult job for me to do since I was the primary vision-bearer and the core of the vision is very close to my heart. The main leader doesn't necessarily have to be the architect behind the vision, but the task should be done by a limited group of leaders who come together for the sole purpose of developing a vision.

The *procedural model* gives a template for how a vision, values, and strategies can be formulated. It is a wonderful and holistic model that includes Christian virtues that work as quality control for the final product. The model is being used in a large number of churches and organizations (see above). It is a rather complex process, but I will mention the first steps of the process in simplified form below.

» The first step is to answer the question "What are our dreams?" Whether it is a leader or a leadership team that answers this question, it is crucial that this process clearly represents the deeply felt convictions of what the leader or leaders want to see. In this phase it isn't necessary to put a lot of energy into the formulations, the main point is to get everything on the table.

» The second step is to reduce the text material you generated in the first step to about half a page.

» The third step is to formulate three or four formal sentences that include a lot of content, written in a way that is easy to remember. At this stage it is probably a good idea to get some help from someone who writes well to help with formulating these sentences.

In light of what we've mentioned earlier, a vision should reflect true, heartfelt, faith-based passions. There must be a sense of direction and hope for the future inherent in the words, as well as reflecting who you are as a church-planting team. If you heart beats faster when you hear the vision, you're definitely on the right track!

I recommend choosing a model – like the one I introduced here – to begin the process of formulating a vision to help you get off to a good start.

M1-5

We believe that what we've written below is one of the most important sections of this book. You will find questions and exercises both for the individual and for those of you who are working as a team. We've also included various case studies for each of the main themes of the book. At the end of the book you'll find a checklist for each of the exercises, as well as the learning goals we had for each of the themes. If you wish to learn more, you can read through the suggested literature list to see if you'd like to order a book for further reading.

The individual exercises, team exercises and case studies are specifically geared for each of the secondary themes of the book. These can be used to generate discussion during team meetings. When used this way, it will be important that each of the team members prepare themselves by going through the material in advance.

The checklist and learning goals are found at the very end of this section. When you go through them, you can chart your own progress: Are we doing what's been suggested, or is it just more head-knowledge for us? Are we working in the intended direction of this chapter? In this way you'll be able to measure your progress against the learning goals of each chapter.

M1-5-1   For chapter M1-1: The kingdom of God and his power – by Øivind Augland

M1-5-1-1   Team exercise 1
Use one of the gatherings with your team to share the dreams you have to start up a new fellowship. Please read the pages on God's dream from Chapter 1.1.3 before meeting together. After sharing with each other, spend 30-45 minutes in prayer with God. Listen to him, who is the Lord of the church, and give him the opportunity to speak into your situation to give his encouragement and guidance.

M1-5-1-2   Team exercise 2
Set aside an evening or two to share your personal testimonies with each other. Use the questions below or something equivalent to share your stories with

each other on the team. After everyone has shared, come around this person and pray for him/her, listening to hear if God wants to speak into their situation. Personal testimonies are likely to contain elements like:

» When did you first meet Jesus?

» Which persons have had the biggest influence on your life – and why?

» How has God influenced and led you in your life?

» What is the most important experience you've had in your life, and why?

» What does it mean for you to follow Jesus today?

M1-5-1-3 Team exercise 3

During the next three months your team is to find ten to fifteen intercessors who will pray regularly for the work you have started. Take time to listen to God and write down the names of those you believe would want to take on this kind of responsibility. Consider how you should ask them, how long you want to challenge them to pray, and how they are to receive information they can pray for.

M1-5-1-4 Individual exercises

» Write down you own personal testimony as a preparation for sharing it with your team.

» Write down the dreams you have for the fellowship you are about to start. What other dreams do you carry within your heart?

» What does it mean to you that God is all-powerful?

» How have you experienced the power of God?

» Have you been able to recruit intercessors for the church planting team? How many have you found, and how will you communicate with them?

» 'In the initial phase of the church-planting ministry, your life and commitment will work to form and influence the new fellowship's culture for a long time to come.' What do you think about this statement?

M1-5-1-5 Case study 1

Carl and Rita are both 28 years old and appointed by their denomination to lead a new church-planting team in a city in Scandinavia with a population of about

10,000. They were born and raised in this city, and they've felt called to plant there for a long time now, and now they're attending a church that is ready to send them out. With them is a team of thirteen young people. They come from a diverse set of backgrounds, but each of them has expressed a desire to start something new. At their first official gathering as a team, Carl and Rita share God's dream to see a new fellowship established. They then challenged the team to share what dreams they carry. During the time of sharing that followed, several of the members express a discontent and criticalness toward their former fellowships and churches. They are definitely looking forward to being part of something better than the past. Carl and Rita feel a bit uncomfortable about the way other churches are spoken about and feel unsure as to how they should tackle the situation.

Describe what you would have done in this situation if you were Carl or Rita.

Why would you deal with the situation the way you describe?

Do you have any biblical support for your reasons?

M1-5-1-6   Case study 2

Peter has been leading a church-planting team for over a year now. His spiritual gift is evangelist. When he started the new fellowship in the area, he was really looking forward to going out with the team to meet people and share the gospel. Before this he had experienced the power of God in amazing ways; he had done street evangelism for several years, had prayed for people, saw many healed and lives changed. But now, a year into the ministry, Peter's frustration is growing. They *had* reached out to new people; they started as a core team with eight people, and now they're over 20 adults divided into three cell groups. Everyone in the core team is involved in the cell groups and is following up new members. Yet at one of the recent team meetings Peter finally exploded: He felt the team was *way* too unconcerned about doing outreach. He was afraid they were all about to turn into introverts, and in his judgment they had lost their focus on God's love for the lost and his desire to reach people. The prayer-walks they had in the area during the first six months had all but shut down. Peter was afraid they were becoming just a cozy little country club and that they didn't think about anyone else but themselves.

How would you analyze the situation described above?

If you were to advise Peter and the core team in this situation, what would you do?

M1-5-2 For chapter M1-2: The church planter – by Øivind Augland

M1-5-2-1 Team exercise 1

Whether they are aware of it or not, every church-planting team chooses a form, a model for their ministry. What kind of expression do you want for your church? What kind of expression do you want 3-5 years from now? Where do you see the same models being used? Would your team be willing to travel to learn from others something that might be important for their ministry? What kind of input do you see your team benefitting from?

M1-5-2-2 Team exercise 2

Go through the questions on "Characteristics of a church planter" together. Reflect on this in relation to your own lives and find some concrete examples of the behavior that is described in the questions. The intention is not to create a feeling of failure; no one ever gets a perfect score on these questions. It is meant to promote reflection on the behavior that is generally necessary in all church planting ministries, especially for the leader. Why do you think those who made these questions considered these areas important? Do you agree that they're important? Are there any other areas you think should be included?

M1-5-2-3 Team exercise 3

Whether you are a team leader or team member, ask yourself this question: Who are you personally accountable to in your life? We would encourage you as team leader to arrange a meeting with the person(s) you choose to be accountable to during the time you are leading the church-planting ministry. (For some of you, this lies within the denominational structure you are a part of). Make an agreement with those you are accountable to as to when and how often you will meet together, what will be important to talk about, and what objectives you have for meeting. Also spend some time talking about your personal commitment (time, resources, and spiritual gifts) in relation to the start-up of the new church. How do you feel the commitment you have towards each other on the team is working?

M1-5-2-4 Individual exercises

» Go through "The characteristics of a church planter." Rate yourself and reflect on the specific situations you've shown the behavior described.

» How would you describe the call you have to be part of starting a new fellowship? How did it happen?

» Are there any others who have confirmed the call you have?

» Spend time praying to the Lord, as well as talk with those closest to you (your spouse and family if you have these) regarding the commitment you have to the fellowship you're about to start.

» Do you have anyone in your life that you have an open and accountable relationship with? Who? Names: _____ If the answer is no, what can you do to find somebody you can be accountable to?

M1-5-2-5 Case study 1

Tim has had a vision to plant a church for some time now. He dreams about planting a church that is relevant to his generation—a church with an expression that speaks to people in their twenties and thirties. He has been youth pastor in the local Pentecostal church for the past five years, and the youth group has really been growing. The church itself is over a hundred years old with about 150 people in attendance on Sunday mornings, located in a college town with about 150,000 inhabitants. The leadership of the church has discussed the subject of church planting for some time now, but a couple of the leaders are still in doubt as to whether or not there is a need for another Pentecostal church in the city. The leadership is aware of the call on Tim's life, but finds the situation difficult. In the end Tim gets a green light from the leadership to gather a core team to plant a new church—the leadership concluded that they actually reach very few of the 6000 students living in the city. So Tim gets started, and sets out building the core team. He plans to spend a year building up the core team to about 30-40 people before starting on setting up a whole lot of programs. He is aware that leaders form the culture of a church, and that they need to spend time together right from the start to build the foundation for this culture.

During one the team meetings, Tim shares his vision for the future and the church model he's found to get them there. He wants to create a relevant service that reaches out to this generation. He is also aware of the importance of smaller groups; so it will be a church with a modern and relevant expression where people also can experience close and warm relationships with each other. After building the core group to 30-40 people within the first year or so, Tim pictures starting up the public services with a goal to reach the twenty- to thirty-year olds in the city's student community. After Tim is done sharing his vision with the team, several questions are raised: "Why such a big focus on the church service? It's all about relationships, right? Maybe we should just build a more organic movement of groups within the city that works its way into the student community? Why can't we just focus on smaller groups that naturally grow and reproduce themselves? Doing church services just demands so much time and money and resources!" There were two members of the core team in particular that spoke quite strongly about these things, and the tensions could be felt growing in the room. Tim feels that they see something different then him and has another model on how the church should look. What he hears them saying doesn't coincide with what he sees and hears from God.

What should Tim as leader do in this situation?

What would you have done if you were confronted with a situation like this?

Discuss this statement: "The model is secondary when you've chosen to start up a new fellowship. The most important thing is to be faithful to the choices you've made, stick to the model you've chosen, and let the consequences of your choices form your work."

M1-5-2-6   Case study 2

Patrick and Tina are married and have led a church-planting team together for two years now. The fellowship has become a group of 30 adults and 25 children. Many people have gotten saved. Patrick has a full-time job on the side while Tina works part-time. They have three children and a year ago they moved into the neighborhood where they're planting the new church. They've worked hard and now they're starting to feel pretty worn out. When they first started they spent a lot of time in prayer—and a lot of time together. But they haven't prayed together the past months except during the leadership gatherings. They feel that they can't really tell all this to the leadership team—they're afraid it might be demotivating. When they started up the work two years ago Patrick and Tina had been challenged to find someone they could meet with as a couple who could hold then accountable in both their personal lives and the development of the ministry. At the time things were going so well they thought, "why on earth do we need somebody like that?" Now they don't have the energy to find help from the outside, even though deep down they know that would be the right thing to do. Patrick and Tina have even started to wonder if they ever really had a call to plant a church. Maybe they never were meant to do this stuff—and maybe they're not meant to continue, either?

You're visiting the new fellowship one day. Patrick and Tina open up to you and tell you about their situation.

How would you approach them?

What do you believe is the right thing for them to do? Why do you think this?

What can you learn from this story in relation to the church-planting ministry you're in?

M1-5-3   For chapter M1-3: Building the core team – by Terje Dahle

M1-5-3-1   Team exercise 1

The core team of the church-planting ministry forms the culture of an emerging fellowship. The ways you relate together, and the things you do as a team, are important. Make a plan for the next six months with the goal of creating a strong and dynamic team for the church-planting ministry. What specific things does your team need to work on? Why are these things important? Set three or four concrete goals that would be important for you to work toward. Make a plan of action based on these.

M1-5-3-2   Team exercise 2

The challenges we meet when we start up a new fellowship can vary from team to team. Ask yourselves in the core team: what will be the three biggest challenges we'll face as the core team in the coming year? Brainstorm together and find ways to prepare for these challenges.

M1-5-3-3   Team exercise 3

Values are those things that are valuable to us. They originate in God and who he is. They guide us in our choices when we are faced with challenges. They create norms for us on how we act individually and corporately. They determine the way we work and do ministry. Our values and actions merge together to form the specific *customs* or *practices* we do in the fellowship. Our values are reflected in who we are and can be recognized in us. It is important that everyone on the team knows the team values and lives in accordance with them. Team decisions based on corporate values are marked with integrity. Our values become the standard we use—not merely to measure others by, but to measure ourselves, our practices and our decisions. Our values protect us from short-term answers and shortcuts that violate what the team agrees on. In this way our values are more than just words, but become the practice of the fellowship, even the *identity* of the fellowship.

What are the values and practices for you and your church-planting team?

M1-5-3-4   Individual exercises

» What is your most important contribution to the team in creating a church culture that is characterized by openness and honesty?

» *Openness in communication*: under this subject you will find six areas that are important for good communication within the team. Reflect on these six areas and ask yourself: How can I help create good communication on the team?

» We have a *function* on the team, not a *position*. We serve with the gifts we have for a higher purpose. Do you understand yourself and the spiritual gifts you have? Are you actively serving with the gifts you have—have you found your place on the team? If not, what can you do about it?

» Tension and conflict are a normal part of any relationship when you live closely with others. What can you do if someone on the team deeply hurts you?

M1-5-3-5   Case study 1

A team of eight people—three couples and two singles—have been sent to plant a church in a relatively new housing area in a city in Norway. The leaders of the team, the married couple Flynn and Pamela, are highly motivated people who worked at a Youth With A Mission base in Mexico for six years before moving to Norway. After a year in the area they had made contact with many people and have seen good things happen. But they haven't seen much growth in the regular attendance at the weekly gatherings.

When the team's advisor meets with them to evaluate their first year, he feels that there isn't a very good spirit of cooperation among them: Some of the team members are talking about moving, while Flynn and Pamela complain about the others' lack of commitment and dedication. The reaction from the others to this is that they see Flynn and Pamela as 'world champions' who clearly seem to get along fine without the rest of them. They feel that they're left out of decision processes and are just given notice about what needs to be done; and they say that they miss a stronger sense of community. When this comes out Flynn becomes defensive and irritated and says that he thought they had come here to *work* and that the kingdom of God is no place for cozy little coffee breaks. He sees the others as passive and feels that nothing would have happened this year if he and Pamela hadn't worked so hard.

How would you, as a team coach, deal with this situation from a team perspective?

What would your response be to Flynn and Pamela?

What would your response be to the rest of the team?

M1-5-3-6   Case study 2

The "Flying Eagle" Church has started a new ministry to establish an independent church in a suburb that is a 45-minute drive from downtown, where the main church has its facilities. The church-planting team has worked together for two years. They are now sitting in a meeting with the leadership of the "Flying Eagle" to look at the next phase of the planting process.

They've seen some new people show up, and about 30-45 people come to the rented storefront for the Sunday afternoon meetings. During the meeting with the "Flying Eagle" leadership, it is mentioned that the core team has seen a lot of people come and go. Tom and Kurt, who've led the ministry since returning from their theology studies in the U.S., feel that it is really hard to get people to make a long-term commitment. It has been especially hard to find people to take responsibility for the various ministry areas. Most of the people from the main church that live in the area are not active in the church planting effort— even those with leadership experience.

Kevin, who leads the main church's prayer ministry but lives in the suburb where the new church is, answers that he already has enough board meetings and committee work when asked why he doesn't get more involved in the new church. But for Kevin, there is something deeper going on: a church is meant to be like a family that loves Jesus and each other – not some sort of church business, like the way Tom and Kurt are running the new fellowship. People don't know each other, and the only thing they have in common is that they happen to live in the same suburb—and very few actually know Tom and Kurt, adds Kevin.

Julie, a young mother who is very involved in the "Flying Eagle", also lives in the area where the church-planting team is working. She says that the high activity level in the new fellowship is not very suitable for young families. A number of others say things like "We don't really know them", "they just seem too perfect for us" and "things just aren't very down-to-earth."

» How would you explain the responses Kevin and Julie give?

» What would your response be to Kevin and Julie?

» What would your response be to Kurt and Tom?

» What would you say to the leadership of the main church?

M1-5-4   For chapter M1-4: Clear vision – by Øystein Gjerme

M1-5-4-1 Team exercise 1: Vision

Spend at least two evenings together as a team to work on questions related to vision.

We actually think you need more than two evenings to work on the vision—but two evenings at least underlines the importance we place on working together to develop a clear vision. If we as leaders of a church-planting team do not paint alternative pictures of what the future could look like, we end up repeating what we already see today. During the process of M4 it is important that someone on the leadership team and core team present a clear picture of where they see the team at a certain point in the future. Spending time together as the core team in prayer and listening to God is important in this vision process. It is always important to have the cultural context in mind when you are working on the vision.

The first evening:

Answer the question: "What are our dreams?" Whether it is the leader or leadership team that answers this question, it is crucial that this process incorporates your deeply felt conviction of what you see for the future. In this phase it is not necessary to put a lot of energy putting your thoughts into proper sentences; the main point is to get everyone's dreams out in the open.

The second evening:

Based on the work from the first evening together you reduce the text material you have to about a half a page. Next is to formulate three or four formal sentences that include a good deal of content while being easy to remember. It might be a good idea to let someone who is good with language to formulate these sentences for the team.

M1-5-4-2 Team exercise 2

Does your church-planting vision make room for the multiplication of new fellowships? Do you see your ministry as something that can reproduce and give birth to new fellowships? Does it make room for further expansion into new areas? It is important to have multiplication in mind when you write down a vision for a fellowship. How can we multiply what we are doing today? In the last part of M4, we will discuss how to plant a movement, fellowship, or church that self-multiplies by starting new movements, fellowships and churches. Is this approach a part of your vision? If not, why? What do you need to do to include it in your vision?

M1-5-4-3   Team exercise 3

Long term goals: Can you specify any long-term goals for your church-planting ministry? What would be important for you to prioritize? Many people in a church-planting ministry report that they want to accomplish more than what resources allow. It is therefore necessary to set some priorities. What is important to prioritize?

Start by making a plan from where you are now to where you will be in two years' time. What should have happened by then? What goals are important to set *now*? What should be your focus as you look forward, and why?

Write down four to six goals for your church-planting team, written as a *two-year timeline*, and then write a plan of action on the timeline to see how and when you will reach these goals.

M1-5-4-4 Individual exercises

» Why do you think this book underlines the importance of having a clear vision when planting something new?

» Someone in the church comes to you and asks: "What is our church's vision—where are we going?" What would answer?

» How would you describe your personal ownership to the vision your team has?

» What is your own perspective on the commitment needed to see your team's vision be realized?

» Has God called you to be part of seeing your team's vision realized?

M1-5-4-5 Case study 1

Ken was one of three people hired by the mother church to lead a church-planting work in a city district four kilometers away. The district has a population of about 5000. Ken moved there with his family and has been engaged in the work for about two years. There were now 20 adults and 15 children in the core group, but the team had regular contact with twice as many. Several of those who joined the new community came from other churches—they had been waiting for something new to happen in the area they lived; so when the new fellowship started they joined the work. After a while people started to think: "Where are we going, anyway? Where do we see ourselves in 10-15 years' time? Our children will be teenagers by then, so have the leaders planned for that? What is actually the vision behind this work?" Ken finds the whole situation a bit difficult, saying, "We're supposed to be a fellowship that wins people to Jesus in the district. Do we really need more than that as our vision?"

What do you think of Ken's reaction?

What can be the reason that Ken reacts like this?

One of the things Ken also says is "I'm not the visionary type. Isn't it more important to look at what's happening in the present?" How would you respond to this?

You are set to guide the leadership in developing a clear vision with long-term goals for the work. How would you proceed? What do you suspect the biggest challenges will be?

M1-5-4-6 Case study 2

Eddy had been the main pastor of a large church with many employees for fifteen years. Many would agree that he is a visionary leader—he always likes looking for new opportunities, is always thinking two steps ahead, and is pretty intense when he speaks about his heart's desires. Many would also agree that he's gifted as an evangelist. Eddy is fully aware of what gifts he's equipped with; he's also aware of his limitations, but always seems to gather people around him to help him in these areas.

A year ago he sensed God call him to move to a neighboring city to start up a new church. He shared this with the leadership. Immediately they found it very difficult to imagine him leaving the church – he was such an important and experienced leader! After praying together, however, they sensed that God was speaking to them, confirming the call for Eddy to plant a new church.

Eddy challenged the church to pay him half his salary for the next two years so that he could plant the new church: the first year he would work 50 % for the church and 50 % with the planting. This was ratified at the church meeting shortly after. He wanted to be accountable to the leadership in the church, and saw a need to mobilize the church in prayer for the new ministry.

He wanted to spend the first year trying to find a core group of 10-15 young families with children. Several of them would probably be people who already lived in the neighboring city, but drove 45 minutes to attend services at the main church. When the core team had been established, he wanted to move his family to the neighboring city. He would spend five years building up a family-oriented church emphasizing the discipleship of children and teenagers. In his dream he saw the creation of a model for family-based churches that could be reproduced in many other cities. Much of the focus would be on smaller family groups meeting in people's homes. After a while they would have corporate gatherings every other week. The gatherings would be a total blast where the kids and young people would be heavily involved in forming the ministry. He had a living picture of how they would fill the civic auditorium with families that would experience that Jesus was relevant in their daily lives.

» From what you read, can you recognize the different elements of the vision that was put in Eddy's heart?

» Describe the vision you believe was in Eddy's mind and dreams.

» How will Eddy's spiritual gifts help him as a leader to accomplish what God has put on his heart?

» Why do you believe the ability to form and communicate a vision is important when starting a new community?

M1-5-5 Learning goals and checklist for church planting

In the following section you will find the learning goals we've made for the different themes covered in these chapters. We would like you now to evaluate yourself and what you've learned. Some of the learning objectives are focused on the acquisition of understanding and knowledge, as well as processing and reflecting on the themes in relation to your own life and team. Other tasks are more concrete, and we believe that they are important for you to work through as a team.

Below you will find the numbers 1 to 5 that you can give as answers according to how well you have worked through the learning objectives. 1 is equivalent to: I have not worked seriously with this objective or looked at the tasks related to it; 5 is equivalent to: I have acquired a good understanding, reflected on, and worked through the tasks related to the learning objective, while 2-4 is somewhere in between. We hope it goes well with your evaluation.

M1-5-5-1 [M1-1 The kingdom of God and his power – by Øivind Augland]

○ ○ ○ ○ ○
1 2 3 4 5
I have acquired a deep understanding that Jesus himself stands behind the building of his church.

○ ○ ○ ○ ○
1 2 3 4 5
I have clarified my personal motives for planting/helping to plant a new fellowship.

○ ○ ○ ○ ○
1 2 3 4 5
I have clarified the dream God has given me to plant/helping to plant a new fellowship.

○ ○ ○ ○ ○
1 2 3 4 5
I understand that the goal is not the church itself, but the expansion of the kingdom of God.

M1-5-5-2 [M1-2 The church planter – by Øivind Augland]

○ ○ ○ ○ ○
1 2 3 4 5

I have a clear understanding of call, sending, and the importance of being in accountable relationships.

○ ○ ○ ○ ○
1 2 3 4 5

I understand the importance of clarifying one's commitment to the core team, both in terms of length of time and in function.

○ ○ ○ ○ ○
1 2 3 4 5

I understand the importance of discovering and ministering according to the gifting God gives a church planter.

○ ○ ○ ○ ○
1 2 3 4 5

I have an understanding of various models of church planting, and have reflected on the various expressions a church plant can have.

M1-5-5-3 [M1-3 Building the core team – by Terje Dahle]

○ ○ ○ ○ ○
1 2 3 4 5

I understand the basis for working in a dynamic team that changes with the tasks and challenges that arise in a church-planting situation.

○ ○ ○ ○ ○
1 2 3 4 5

I understand the importance of values and value-based practices that characterize the culture of a new fellowship.

○ ○ ○ ○ ○
1 2 3 4 5

I understand the need for developing an open, honest, and healthy communication within the team, and understand how conflicts arise.

M1-5-5-4 [M1-4 Clear vision – by Øystein Gjerme]

○ ○ ○ ○ ○
1 2 3 4 5

I understand the importance of having a clearly written vision in a church-planting ministry.

○ ○ ○ ○ ○
1 2 3 4 5

I understand the importance of making a plan for how and when the core leadership team should create a clear vision for a church-planting ministry.

○ ○ ○ ○ ○
1 2 3 4 5

I understand the importance of a goal-directed ministry, and of starting the process of developing long-term goals with an action plan for the first two years of the work.

"Therefore go..."

Mission

M2-
MISSION
- Therefore
go!

M2-0

INTRODUCTION – BY ØIVIND AUGLAND

[197] Roxburgh, Allan J, and Romanuk, Fred. *The Missional Leader, Equipping your Church to Reach a Changing World.* San Francisco: Jossey-Bass, 2006 (p xv).

[198] John 17:18

[199] Stetzer, Ed. *Planting Missional Churches.* Nashville, TN: Broadman & Holman Publishers, 2006.

The second part of the Great Commission says, "Therefore go!" Being a church is about being on God's mission.[197] Church planting is *mission*. If we don't reach out to new people, we will still be the same group of people in 3-5 years. Many church plants have unfortunately become small, introverted groups that no longer reach out to new people. Church planting is about planting the Good News in a geographic area, culture, or ethnic group, with the goal to reach the unreached with the gospel. We carry the kingdom of God within us and are sent by the King of Kings. We are called to build his dwelling place in this world, a place where he can dwell and reveal himself to people.

We are a part of God's *sending* to this world. Just as God sent his only Son into the world, he sends you into this world to present the Kingdom of God to people who don't know him.[198] All church planting takes place from an understanding of call and sending. In M1 we touched on the themes of call and vision. It is important to know that you are called and what you are called to build (vision). It is also be important for you to know to whom you are sent. Being *missional* is about planting a church in a group or culture you have been called to reach.[199] The questions you must ask are "what is the target group we are trying to reach? Are we sent to a specific area? Are we called to a clearly defined group or are we to bring the Kingdom of God to a group for which few have been reached by the gospel?" It is essential that you have a clear idea of who you are sent to. Øystein Gjerme brings this up in the first theme "Pioneering and comfort zones."

Church planting is pioneer work, and it challenges our comfort zones. Church planting is a choice that affects many parts of our lives. It challenges our relationships. I clearly remember a comment from one of the central persons on the team that planted Hånes Free Church. He went with us from the mother church with his family and had this reflection: "Now that I've joined this church-planting team, I need to give up some good relationships that were built through the years, so that I can have the time and space needed to invest in new relationships and be friends with new people." There are many reasons why a person comes to a church, but only one reason why they stay – *they've become friends with someone in the church.* Church planting will take you beyond your comfort zone by continuously offering friendship to new people. It will challenge your finances, your family life, and how you prioritize your time and resources. But remember what Jesus said, "I am with you always." We are not sent out alone; he is with us. It is a privilege to be part of his mission to this world.

Church planting is mission. What does it mean for you as a core team to be *missional*? When church planting is built on sharing the Good News, we have to see that we *are* the Good News. The kingdom of God lives in us; where we are, God will be. We are his hands, feet, ears, and mouth to our neighborhood—the Good News is present in *your* neighborhood because *you* live there. Mission is no not an activity but a life we live. "God's love has been poured out into our hearts through the Holy Spirit, who has been given to us."[200] "For Christ's love compels us, because we are convinced that one died for all, and therefore all died. And he died for all, that those who live should no longer live for themselves but for him who died for them and was raised again."[201] It is Christ's love within us that makes the difference. You have what is needed. Arne Skagen addresses this in his chapters: "Loved and Sent" and "The Harvest Is Ripe."

Jesus had to bring correction to the disciples by saying, "Don't you have a saying, `It's still four months until harvest'? I tell you, open your eyes and look at the fields! They are ripe for harvest."[202] We often have a tendency to think "some time in the future", while Jesus says that the harvest is ripe *today.* Now, today, you will be in touch with a harvest that is ripe—people who are open and ready to receive the gospel, open to receive God's love through you. A ripe grain field doesn't walk into the barn on its own; the farmer has to go out and harvest the grain. People who are open to the gospel do not come to the church alone, you

[200] Romans 5:5

[201] 2 Corinthians 5:14-15

[202] John 4:35

[203] Romans 1:16

[204] Romans 15:18-19

have to go out and meet their needs, pray for them, become friends with them, share the gospel with them, and lead them into the kingdom of God and the community of faith. This is what it means to be *missional*.

We've often heard it said that the way of the gospel today is: "Belong – Believe – Behave." A sense of belonging, relationships, and friendships are very important when we share the gospel with people. But we must also underline the fact that "friendship saves no one" – it is the gospel of Jesus Christ that is "the power of God that brings salvation to everyone who believes."[203] In Norway and Europe we've seen that it is only when God is experienced in a friendship that things begin to happen. Arnt Jakob Holvik brings this up in the last part of "M2 - Mission."

The apostle Paul sums up his apostolic service and describes how he preached the gospel by saying: "I will not venture to speak of anything except what Christ has accomplished through me in leading the Gentiles to obey God by what I have said and done – by the power of signs and wonders, through the power of the Spirit of God. So from Jerusalem all the way around Illyricum, I have fully proclaimed the gospel of Christ." [204]

When the gospel is "fully proclaimed", it is done in both word and action with signs and wonders following-- everything done through the power of the Spirit with this one goal in mind: to lead the peoples of the world to obedience. This is the apostolic preaching of the gospel that made such an impact during Paul's time and that will make an impact on ours. The gospel must be preached in *word* so people can get saved, but it also has to be demonstrated through good deeds that convey the love of Jesus in a practical way. On top of all this the gospel has to be made visible through signs and wonders: we offer to pray for people who are sick, set people free from the past and raise up those who are down. This can only take place when we let the Holy Spirit lead us in the things we do.

If you are anything like me, other things can so easily grab my attention from doing the important things described above. In church planting we need to make ourselves accountable to each other on how we spend our time building relationships with the unsaved. In this matter it can be a good idea to be a bit strategic.

Ask God to show you which group of people your team should focus on first. Then pray about, reflect on and identify the *arenas* where you can meet these people. Examples of arenas are youth centers, existing social networks, cafés, the streets, organized sports, or the neighborhood. But your team can also *create* such arenas: organize an international lunch for immigrants; hold an Alpha Course; plan activities for the children in the neighborhood, etc. There are a lot of opportunities to meet people and build relationships with them.

Take time listening to God as a team, asking him to reveal to you those people who are ripe for the harvest that you are already touching somehow—and then keep each other accountable to act. Commit yourselves as a fellowship to individually pray for two or three people you believe are open for the gospel. In the team exercises and case studies found in this section of the book, you will be challenged to be strategic and practical when planning how the fellowship you are planting can reach out to new people.

M2-1

PIONEER WORK AND COMFORT ZONES – BY ØYSTEIN GJERME

[205] Barker, Joel Arthur. *Paradigms: The Business of Discovering the Future.* NewYork: Harper Business, 1994.

[206] Genesis 2:15

[207] Genesis 3:1-24

[208] Genesis 3:1-24

[209] Genesis 3:1-24

M2-1-1   Introduction

Church planting is entrepreneurial work and demands an unusual kind of effort and commitment. Futurist Joel Barker categorizes people by looking to the different types of people who pioneered America's Wild West. First to come were the *trailblazers,* who were willing to take great risks to tame the Wild West. There weren't many of them, and they worked completely alone until the land was a bit safer for others. The next group to head west was the *pioneers*; they cleared the land and built homesteads knowing that wild animals and potential dangers were always nearby. The third group, which was the majority, was the *settlers* who arrived only after the pioneers had sent word that it was safe enough to start building cities. [205]

Church planters are trailblazers and pioneers, driven by an urge to reach new areas and establish new churches. This urge originates from God's commission to the world and the church planter's commitment to the call of God.

M2-1-2   The mission of God

M2-1-2-1   Missio dei

God created a good world; he made man and woman so he could share his life with them, and they with each other. He made things in a way that man and woman would express his glory in the world by working its land and taking care of it.[206] This harmony was disturbed when the force of evil confused the man and woman, allowing evil to enter the world.[207] Because of the fall, Adam and Eve lost their relationship with God and stopped serving him in creation. They and their descendants carried the fall with them, something that becomes obvious in the cultures they established around them. Society became filled with violence, hatred, greed, abuse, idolatry and confusion.[208] And then God decided to save the world.[209]

To be able to save the world God had to involve himself in the history of man. His first move was to involve himself in the life of the people of Israel. In the relationship between God and Israel we can see images and examples that are marked with signs of what is to come. By becoming human through Jesus Christ, and by his life, death, and resurrection, God rescues the world from the power of evil.[210]

This is a short summary of *Missio Dei*, the missionary activity of God. It is a central biblical theme that describes the purpose of God's actions in history.[211] He is the one who sends the church into the world to complete his work of salvation and, as we explained earlier, to accomplish his dream of establishing churches in every corner of the world. The church planter clears the way and is a pioneer in places and cultures where there have never been churches before. The church planter clears the way by following his or her own call and calls out to others to join in the building of the church.

M2-1-2-2 The church is "called out"

The word *church* is translated from the Greek word *ekklesia*. This word is mainly found after the death and resurrection of Jesus, and it means *a gathering of believers*. In the Greek translation of the New Testament, the Septuagint, the *ekklesia* was used to describe the gathering of God's people in the context of meeting for special religious purposes.[212] The word was also used to describe an official political gathering in Greek society.[213] The sum of the different historical usages of the word tells us that the church is a gathering of people. *Ekklesia* is put together by the words *ek* "out from" and *kaleo* "called". Even though it is unclear whether or not the etymology was in the minds of those who wrote the New Testament, it is inferred from the context that precisely those who were "called out" who were considered to be the church.

It is being "called out" from the stream that others follow, and instead choosing to follow God with their whole lives, that the church planter and church-planting team find their identity. God sends a group of people into an area to build a local church, which is the great privilege and challenge of the church planter. The group that rallies together to plant a church must know who they are sent to.

M2-1-2-3 Who are we sent to?

God's great plan to send Jesus and the "called" church to the world is made real and set in motion by every single church-planting ministry. It is up to every church-planting team to define what their church should look like based on the culture they're bringing the Good News to. You can't escape a thorough cultural analysis if you want to reach the people you're targeting. At the same time, while

[210] John 1:1-14; Philippians 2:6-11; Colossians 1:13-22

[211] Guder, Darrell L. *Missional Church.* Grand Rapids: Eerdmans, 1998 (p 4).

[212] Deuteronomy 9:10; 18:16; 23:1-3

[213] Acts 19:32, 39-40

[214] Malm, Magnus.
I lammets tegn,
p 155.

[215] Guder, 223.

doing your cultural analysis, you have to have an understanding of the missional church so that your analysis doesn't become an isolated exercise. Magnus Malm, in his book "The Sign of the Lamb," warns churches against making the needs of society the motivating force of the church; the church can become marginalized if it bases it existence solely on conditions set by society.

In the end, it is the resurrected Christ, and not the efforts of the church, which is the answer to the problems of our time. The church must stand before Jesus in such a way that allows him to work through it in reaching the world—while assuring that the world can still see Jesus behind it all. The church must be careful not to get in the way of the world seeing Jesus in its attempts at being "relevant".[214]

There is an imminent danger of "mission drift" in all cross-cultural missions, when the message is in danger of being blurred through the church's efforts in reaching a new group. This can be prevented by keeping a missional interpretation of the Bible, allowing us to see how integral mission is in the biblical narrative.

M2-1-2-4 Missional biblical interpretation

The first Christians did mission while receiving guidance through the epistles and texts that we now refer to as the New Testament. The purpose of the texts was to help the churches to continue their mission despite their circumstances, challenges, and battles. Church planters often experience that the Bible becomes more alive, not just as a source of information, but also as a source of inspiration in finding ways of communicating the message to people in unreached cultures. From this perspective you can see how Scripture motivates and underlines the church's mission, being the guarantor that there is always "more land to conquer."[215]

In conflicts that arise in the interface of the church with our secular, postmodern, neo-pagan culture, there are plenty of problems and challenges to threaten "right biblical teaching." Øivind Augland and Håvard Kjøllesdal bring up the subject in M3 "Multiplication" under the theme "Making disciples in today's culture." In an established church organization the distance to this sort of culture can be so great that the issues here can be considered theoretical. My experience is that church planting will lead you directly into these issues and force you to consider them. The good news is that every page of the epistles of the New Testament was written in the same crossfire, and they are of great help on the missional journey.

M2-1-2-5 Who is the target group?

When we planted the Salt Church of Bergen in 2004, we wanted to build a church for the ordinary people of Bergen. We decided not to plant a church as a reaction against the Pentecostal background we came from, but we still had to get an idea as to how our target group was different from our work in the Pentecostal church. Here are some of the questions that helped us get an idea of what kind of culture we wanted to reach:

» What is the age group of the people we want to reach?

_____

_____

_____

_____

» What knowledge do they have of the Christian faith?

_____

_____

_____

_____

» What is their understanding and attitude toward the term "church"?

_____

_____

_____

_____

» What does a typical day look like for a family with small children in our target group?

_____

_____

_____

216 Ibid.

» What needs do our target group have?

_____

_____

_____

_____

» What will attract their attention?

_____

_____

» What could make it easier for us to come in contact with them?

_____

_____

Here is the short version of the answers our team gave to the above questions:

»   The people are 20-40 years old, young adults and families with small children.

»   We aim for people without a lot of knowledge of the Christian faith, and we aim to find a language and culture that includes both those with a Christian background and those without.

»   It is a place for those who are especially religiously interested.[216]

»   A place with a lot of things going on!

»   Relevant communication of the gospel will take into consideration the felt needs of the people.

»   A healthy, modern, and up-to-date church where people freely choose their level of involvement.

»   Caring relationships.

That was our starting point, but things can change along the way. We've discovered that:

» In the 20-40 age group, very many choose to have children, and the children's work in the church is both demanding and defining for the church culture.

» We must repeatedly remind the church of why we use language and culture as tools to reach our target group.

» We must continuously struggle to prevent an internal church culture from emerging where we find ourselves content with being a mediocre church.

» We must continuously challenge "the busyness culture" by presenting church work as a privilege and not a punishment.

» We must continuously seek to be relevant and in touch with real life in our preaching and in our LIFE group discussions, even though it is a genuine temptation to dive deep into some of the subjects that attract the attention of those who are especially religiously interested.

» We must regularly adjust the way we communicate what we expect from people in the church. When we try to do too much, we increase our expectations on people and set the stage for group pressure that the postmodern individualist immediately runs away from.

» We must always hold relationships high and encourage the church to spend time together and to include others.

» It's become totally clear to us that a strong focus on the target group is a good thing, but it comes with an unexpected price that isn't seen until later: The more some church members love the church culture, the more others despise it. And you have to be prepared to handle that tension.

» It is a fantastic privilege being a trailblazer and a pioneer, sent into new cultures and places. But this privilege requires constant commitment.

[217] Luke 14:28-32

[218] Augland, Øivind. *Organization and organism.* 2011 (Notes on the various developmental phases of a church).

M2-1-3   Commitment

M2-1-3-1   The cost of discipleship

Church planting is a long-term project, and before you decide to go ahead with it, you have to count the cost of what it takes to do it. Jesus said something related to the cost of discipleship:

> "Suppose one of you wants to build a tower. Won't you first sit down and estimate the cost to see if you have enough money to complete it? For if you lay the foundation and are not able to finish it, everyone who sees it will ridicule you, saying 'this person began to build and wasn't able to finish.' Or suppose a king is about to go to war against another king. Won't he first sit down and consider whether he is able with ten thousand men to oppose the one coming against him with twenty thousand? If he is not able, he will send a delegation while the other is still a long way off and will ask for terms of peace." [217]

It takes 4-7 years before a church-planting effort can be declared finished. Every church planter has to expect to be totally involved in the work during this phase to ensure that the fellowship survives. The need for a huge investment of time doesn't stop after the initial start-up phase, but continues into the following phases as well. The various phases in an organization's development can be described as follows: the pioneer phase, the structure phase, the delegation phase, and the coordination phase. Each of these phases is marked with its own characteristics that a church planter needs to be aware of.[218]

A resounding "yes" to the investment of time and resources in a church-planting ministry also means a resounding "no" to other priorities. The reward of seeing a new church come to life has to outweigh the costs involved in making it happen. It is wise to work in consultation with your spouse in what to say "yes" and "no" to in planting a church, since your choices will affect nearly all aspects of your personal life.

M2-1-3-2   Prioritizing the rhythm of time

First of all, church planting will affect the way you spend your time. The nature of pioneer work is that it happens outside of normal working hours. It is passion that thrusts a new idea to life, and passion finds a way of making things happen—usually requiring major amounts of effort. An awareness of how time is spent can secure a balance between work and rest. Because establishing a church is a long-term commitment, it is crucial to find as early as possible a working rhythm that won't wear you down. These issues are further addressed in the last two themes of M4 "Movement."

Early in our planting process we worked out what our weekly rhythm should look like. After spending four months together in a DNA-fellowship with the core group of around 40 people, we started up services every Sunday in the pre-phase before the church was officially opened. It was important to establish this early in the church planting, since we were planting in a big city and the Sunday service is an important part of our church expression.

Because we planted during a phase when people in leadership had small children, it was important that we scheduled our leadership meetings outside the hours 16:00-20:00. Children come home from school and pre-school at that time, and family life needs tending then. So we intentionally planned our weekly meetings between 20:00-22:00. We specifically planned that only two weekdays be "Salt Church of Bergen Days"— with leadership meetings on Mondays and cell group meetings on Wednesdays. In this way we've been able to control the amount of time used for church and keep activity levels low, consistent with our church values.

Meeting at a regular place has been very useful for us. Some say that this could be done more informally through weekly invitations and by using the grapevine. But we think that a more-informal structure exposes the church-planting team to a high degree of wear and tear. In desiring to be organic and relational, a lot of church-planting teams inadvertently limit the number of people they can reach out to by appearing less organized and available to those outside the core group (the very people they are trying to reach out to), which discourages those outside from joining the group. It is the opposite of what the team intends, but this is the result of choosing the wrong church model for a target group living in a very organized and regulated part of the world.

Having services every Sunday at a set time has been a strength for our ministry; the leaders, with very few exceptions, have been present at all meetings. Our dream is to raise up Sundays as church-service days again in our country, and we challenge our leaders to lead the way as good examples.

M2-1-3-3 Relationships before activities

Second, church planting affects your social orientation. It is a great pleasure to spend time with the ones you build a church with, and it is absolutely necessary if you want to create secure relational bonds. But when you choose to spend time with someone, you choose *not to* spend time with others. It is a "cost of opportunity" you are forced to make as church planters. And by "forced" I mean because of the ministry, not because something is imposing it on you. It is a sobering thought to acknowledge that this may take time away from your family, friends, and others who are not on the church planting team.

In light of this, it is important to speak about these things, and explain the priorities you make in relation to your family, friends, and extended family. Without clarifying this you risk the possibility of conflicts and feelings of loss with the ones you love that in turn can sap you of your energy.

M2-1-3-4 Taking care of your own family

Third, church planting affects the inner dynamics of the church planter's family. The family often hosts gatherings in their own home, and is expected to be "on" whenever people come to the house. They also must live with the fact that the church planter often brings work home—both spiritually and mentally. Even though these pressures vary from leader to leader, it is important to find smart solutions to simplify the situation. Our experience is that when we can meet this potential conflict with a "win-win" and not a "win-lose" attitude, we've come far.

For us, it all started during our time as students when we discussed what the future might hold for us. My wife worried about how church planting could affect marriage and family, and we discussed what would come in first, second, and third place with respect to God, family, and church. We never arrived at a clear answer, but we found the answer when someone told us "God never makes this kind of list. He invites us to have everything in first place, to have a life that includes all of these." This statement has helped us ever since. We have one life, and there is room for all to win. To show you how we practice this, let me mention the example of holding leadership meetings in our home.

If we have a meeting in our own home, we always let the children participate during the first part of the meeting. Interaction between the leaders and our children was a conscious choice in creating a culture where the children feel included and significant. Because we are hosting a function of the church in our own home, someone always comes early to help us with the preparations, and everyone helps to clean up before saying goodbye and going home. All our key leaders are very grateful that we established this culture of meeting in our homes, now that they have meetings with other leaders in their own homes. This is a win-win situation for all parts, and it makes it easier to be a host in our hectic daily lives.

Pioneer work is all consuming, and the financial, relational, and social costs can be demanding if you don't set healthy limits for yourself. As the observant reader probably has recognized, setting healthy limits is already an inherent part of the church culture I have described above. We believe that setting limits is not so much about saying "no" as it is about saying "yes" to the right choices and priorities. The limits you set should therefore be founded on values and a common understanding of what is best for everyone in the long run. An approach like this builds a culture of respect for each other, which again frees the leaders from having to make countless choices all the time.

M2-1-4 Out of the comfort zone

Planting a church is a choice that affects many parts of your life. While most people choose to become established in the work place in order to receive financial security, a sense of belonging to a place, and healthy balance in their personal resource bank, church planters often do the exact opposite. Not only do church planters have to take care of their own finances, their own sense of belonging, and management of their personal resources—they have to take care of everyone who follows them, too!

M2-1-4-1 Uncertain finances

Financial resources are a crucial premise for succeeding as a church planter. Having a lot of money or little is irrelevant; the vital part is to manage the funds one has by principles that originate in the kingdom of God. The church planter must manage the finances of the church as well as his own personal finances. But it begins in the private sphere where you receive more than enough opportunities to have your comfort zone challenged.

I was taught an important lesson about responsibility when I was a student in Minneapolis, Minnesota, USA and had a performance appraisal with the pastor I worked for. He asked me how my finances were, and I answered that my bank account was nearly empty, but I had faith in God. He looked straight at me and said, "You may experiment with the power of your faith when you're single. But now you are a married man and are responsible for your wife." Then he took all the banknotes he had in his wallet, gave them to me and started to teach me about living in financial responsibility by faith before God. This experience, together with all the other teachings I've received through the years, have formed my personal conviction of the importance of the financial principles found in the kingdom of God.

The insight I have based on personal experience form the way I look at finances in church planting. If we do our part, God will always do his part to provide financial security. This kind of security is important when you feel like things are going the wrong direction or when access to financial resources is limited. It is at times like these that you have to have your comfort zone firmly established in a vibrant life of faith in God and his promises.

M2-1-4-2 Correct prioritizing

Another crucial premise to succeed in your church-planting ministry is to be proactive in managing your time. I use the term "to manage your time" deliberately to underline that time can either be managed—or be the manager. Different personality types cope differently with time pressure, and I can only give some examples from my own life, categorized with the help of Stephen Covey's Quadrant Model for Time Management.

	NOT URGENT	URGENT
IMPORTANT	1. PLANNING » Relationships » Maintenance » Relaxation » Things with value » Structures and good habits	2. CRISIS » Chaos, stress » Dead lines » Meetings » Necessary initiatives – NOW » Disease » Poor maintenance
NOT IMPORTANT	3. TIME THIEVES » Junk mail » Texting or too much small talk » TV and media » Distractions	4. DELEGATING » Some email » Activities others can do » Certain appointments

It is helpful to use these quadrants long enough for you to learn how to sort tasks into a healthy pattern like this. After you've established this habit, you won't need to spend much time thinking about it.

M2-1-4-3 Living against the stream

Church planting is like doing missions work in our own back yard—and the contrast to other people's secular workday and priorities becomes very clear. A church planter goes in the opposite direction of most others; and the risks you are exposed to in being a church planter may tempt you to choose to do something else. Temptation has many faces; but I'd like to focus on the particular temptation that goes with the feeling of "going against the stream."

In Scandinavia there are two questions you normally ask when you meet somebody new. The first is, "What's your name?" and the second one is "What do you do for a living?" Our identity lies mostly in what we do, and a career-oriented culture doesn't exactly look up to church planters or place us high on the status rankings. Appreciation and respect must solidly be anchored in the church planter's identity, returning to the conviction of his or her calling when faced with the expectations of others.

Disagreements, tensions, and conflicts can arise in all phases of church planting. This can be explained in the terminology of organizational psychology— and/or with spiritual explanatory models. During these processes, there is usually someone who decides to leave or end their time of service—something that may trigger a sense of loss or rejection in a church planter. When these things happen it is important to remember that situations like these happen to every leader, regardless of who that leader is. It is good to practice sorting through these situations; having a person to speak freely with can help in this process.

The road to achieving your church-planting goals can seem long at times; and, when your private life goes through change—such as when a new baby comes—your original passion for the ministry may come in conflict with other obligations. In these situations it is important that people who provide support and supervision for the church planter catch these signals early, so that necessary efforts are implemented to help the leader regain his or her focus in order to regain their energy.

In church planting there are many other temptations and challenges along the way that can make it seem very attractive to end the whole church-planting project. It can be hard to mobilize volunteers, difficult to secure the necessary financial resources, conflicts between others in the church that feel threatened by the church planting ministry, personal challenges, and personal doubt in your own capacity and abilities. In the situations mentioned above, there are two ways out: Either you can run and hide, or you can challenge your own comfort zone by aiming for personal development and growth to help you get through it.

M2-1-5   Sent out together

M2-1-5-1   The role of the leader

In M1 – "Master" I wrote on the subject of who you are sent to, and Terje Dahle wrote about how to build a core team. Terje mentioned the importance of the composition and dynamics of the team. With challenging our comfort zone in mind, I will briefly draw attention to some other perspectives on the subject.

Church planting is only possible when a group of people agree to focus their energies on working together toward a common goal. My personal opinion is that the church planter is the bulldozer during the church's establishment. A leader is not a leader unless someone follows him. The way people follow the leader differs in different phases of church planting.

In the pioneer phase the leadership takes on a directive style of leadership. The leader directs choices and priorities, securing progress for the work. In this phase the leader's presence and clarity in communication function as the team's executive authority, demanding undivided attention from the team members.

In the phases that follow – the structure phase, the delegation phase, and the coordination phase – the leadership style changes in proportion to growth rates in the church-planting ministry. During these phases ministries are developed, mandates are given, responsibilities are delegated, and so on. A church planter who finds it difficult making room for others to work will find it challenging just to keep up with the status quo—and risks suffocating the emerging church before it even gets started. Yet it is a known fact that many church planters make this very mistake. The mistake doesn't only have practical consequences for the team; it is also a violation of the foundational identity of the church as the "fellowship of those who are called." We will return to this later.

Within my own church context, our supervisors and counselors have been decisive in helping our main leaders understand these dynamics. Because of this we have constantly prioritized choosing, training, and developing a high number of leaders who have been made ready to take on greater responsibility as the church moves into subsequent phases of development.

Understanding this must first come from the main team leader, who must allow the perspectives of others to give guidance to the team. One of our supervisors once warned me that the rate of the development of new leaders was too low in one of our departments, remarking that, "You will experience trouble in 12-18 months' time if you don't do something about this now." We did something about it and managed to avoid a crisis in the department that in the end would have affected the whole church. The important thing is to understand that church planting is about releasing people into ministry so that we can build the church *together*.

M2-1-5-2 The role of the team

There are many theories on how a team should be put together, and I can only share what we've experienced as important. First of all, I make sure that there's good chemistry between the leaders, so that we can work together in an orderly and considerate manner. Related to this is thinking about the specific team functions you need, and then fill these functions according to those needs. The challenge with this approach is that you end up only recruiting people for their *skills*. We believe that skills can be trained, while the relational chemistry and attitudes on the team are much harder to form.

As the work grows and more people join and various ministry teams are created to run the church, forming teams according to skills and functions becomes less of a risk. At one point it is totally necessary that certain types of people be represented in a team to ensure stability and progress.

A foundational principle for working together as a leadership team is that each member believes in the motives, model, and method of the main leader. There should be a basic trust in the leader's motives in being a church planter, and this should hold even in challenging circumstances. In modern church life there are many models to form a church by, so it is important that the team remains loyal to the model they started with. The choice of model determines the method you use to build the church—that is, the practical execution of church work based on the combined vision, values and strategies of the church. Here in Scandinavia, where the culture is strongly influenced by the concepts of equality and consensus, the team needs to reconcile their particular attitudes towards leadership in order to clarify the team's expectations for the person functioning as architect of the pioneering work. Disagreement around the leadership's structure and authority is unfortunately the background for many of the challenges found in church planting.

M2-1-5-3 How to build a team

It takes a strong team to build a church that lasts. Well into the planting of the church, I told my closest leaders that I didn't need a *planting* team—I needed a *destiny* team! There is a description of how to build a good team: STAR. This acronym stands for: *Skills, Teachability, Authority,* and *Relationship.*[219]

Skills: Skills can be taught, but team members have to come with a willingness to learn new skills, adding to the ones they brought with them to the team. But you rarely create specialists on a church planting team; instead, you provide your team members with a broad spectrum of leadership experience. It's been important for me to make sure that none of our leaders "own" a task or department, but is flexible enough to fill the needs that are necessary to fill.

Teachability: A condition for personal growth is nurturing a teachable attitude, one of the best preventative medicines against self-importance, competition and complacency. A team worker must live in a state of personal renewal and learning, finding joy in the presence of masters.

Authority: Those who are under authority practice authority. Equality-based cultures—like those in Scandinavia—have a particular need to lay a biblical foundation for how authority is handled. Those who approach authority honorably will in turn be honored by those they have authority over.

Relationship: Team relationships don't grow on their own, but are formed over time through intentional involvement with each other. Strengthening the chemistry on a team requires stepping out of our team roles and getting to know each other under other circumstances, allowing our comfort zones to be challenged.

The strength of the leadership team is an indicator of the strength of the church. Spending time and resources to strengthen the core team is a good investment for the entire church. And, if there is anyone in the church who should know the call on your life, it should be those in your core team. The Bible makes it clear that God is a *sending* God, and that he sends people *together*.

[219] Wilson Scott developed parts of this model, but the copyright for the acronym is unknown.

M2-1-6 Summary

Pioneer work challenges our personal comfort zones in many different ways. In this short text I have highlighted a few of these ways to stimulate your reflection as a church planter. You know your own comfort zones best, and so I invite you to be aware of them as you go out and make disciples in the places you are sent.

M2-2

LOVED AND SENT – BY ARNE SKAGEN

220. Joshua 1:9

221 John 17:18

222 See Matthew 10:40 and John 13:20

M2-2-1   Introduction

We are sent by God with a mission. These are the basics: When we receive Jesus we are born into the kingdom of God. And then we are sent out *with* the kingdom of God—everything that God has to offer: His love, peace, power and authority.

God doesn't send us on a mission and then leave us out there to fend for ourselves; the Great Commission—to go into all the world with the good news, baptize and disciple people—is Mission Impossible – *for us*, but not for God. "I am with you always," ensures Jesus in Matthew 28 after he gave the mission to his disciples.

God said exactly the same to Moses when he sent him to free the Israelites from captivity in Egypt. Then when Joshua was called to take over Moses' leadership position and lead the people into the Promised Land, he heard something similar: "Have I not commanded you? Be strong and courageous. Do not be afraid; do not be discouraged, for the Lord your God will be with you wherever you go."[220] "I am with you always." Jesus is with us and in us, through his Spirit.

In the gospel of John, Jesus says more than forty times that he was sent by God. And in the same way—says Jesus – are we, his followers, sent. "As you sent me into the world, I have sent them into the world." [221]

Jesus had no doubt about who sent him. We as Christians need to live in a fresh revelation that we are sent, and who it is who sends us. "Those who receive you, receive me," says Jesus. "Those who listen to you, listen to me." [222]

This statement has to mean that when you share the gospel with people and they listen to you – they're actually listening to Jesus! When they receive us, they receive Jesus.

"But I just don't know what to say or do with people who aren't walking with Jesus!" you might complain, in your own little mind. "I just get so nervous and just have so much—*fear of man*!" Relax! You are not alone in thinking or feeling this way. A lot of people are just like you. Just remember that the *Holy Spirit* isn't nervous; there isn't one ounce of *fear of man* in him! The Holy Spirit wants to

223 Luke 4:18-21;
Isaiah 61:1-2

224 John 14:12

teach us how to cooperate with him when we meet others. He'll help us to fear *God*, not people. Don't let fear tell you what you can and cannot do, say or not say. Instead, let yourself be led by the Spirit – the Advocate and Counselor who dwells in you. We have to remember that Jesus came to this earth and became just like us—except without sin. But he was just as dependent on the Holy Spirit as you and I are. Acts 10:38 talks about "how God anointed Jesus of Nazareth with the Holy Spirit and power, and how he went around doing good and healing all who were under the power of the devil, because God was with him."

Okay. So we're *sent*. But what's the mission? What are we sent to *say and do*?

When Jesus stood in front of the synagogue in his hometown of Nazareth at the beginning of his public ministry, he opened the scroll and read from the prophet Isaiah: "The Spirit of the Lord is on me, because he has anointed me to proclaim good news to the poor. He has sent me to proclaim freedom for the prisoners and recovery of sight for the blind, to set the oppressed free, to proclaim the year of the Lord's favor."

Then he rolled up the scroll and said, "Today this scripture is fulfilled in your hearing." [223]

We are sent to do the same things that Jesus did. [224] Our mission is to preach the good news, set the captives free, give the blind their sight and proclaim the year of the Lord's favor.

This can only happen when we live our lives filled with the Spirit of Jesus, understand who we are in him and what we have in him, and when we learn to work with the Holy Spirit each day.

M2-2-2 Driven by love

M2-2-2-1 The kingdom of God at the retirement home

Sara works at a retirement home. She's prayed for many years for the people who live in the home. Sara loves these old people and one day her love drives her to do something about it. She walks up to the manager of the retirement center and asks if it would be okay for her to invite some friends over from church to talk with the old people – and to pray for them.

The manager was a bit surprised by this, but answered that yes, it would be okay. "—As long as it all happens in a dignified manner," he added.

I'm a friend of Sara's, and one of the two friends who one day got to go with her to the retirement home.

It can be really interesting meeting people who've lived long lives. A lot of them have a lot to talk about. At the same time – when we get closer to them – a number of them will tell you that they get a bit anxious when they think about the future. They've reached the average life expectancy; the retirement home, for all intents and purposes, could be their last stop. What happens then? Is there anything more to hope for?

We talk with the people and share the gospel with them. We tell them about God's plan of salvation, why Jesus came and what he came to give: *a future and a hope*. A few of the people are touched by God's love, a tear can be seen in an eye or two around the room. Others grasp our hands and tell us how glad they are that we came.

At one of the tables sits a lady named Judith. She's followed carefully what's been said about the gospel. When we ask her what she thinks about what we shared, she replies,

"I believe."

We sit ourselves around the table, take out a Bible and read a verse to her:

"If you declare with your mouth, "Jesus is Lord," and believe in your heart that God raised him from the dead, you will be saved."

"Do you want to receive Jesus?" we ask.

"Yes, I do!" replies Judith, loud and clear. And in simple words she invites Jesus into her heart.

Judith is the first to get saved, but not the last: that morning five others do the same.

With Sara as a natural gathering point, the old people begin to meet for prayer, Bible study, coffee drinking and socializing. It happens a couple of times a week, in a retirement home somewhere on the west coast of Norway.

[225] John 3:16

[226] Romans 5:5

[227] 2 Corinthians 5:14

M2-2-2-2 God's love poured out into our hearts

The story of Sara at the retirement home shows us what the driving force must be for all evangelism: the love of God.

God loves people. God loves all people, with a love that was willing to sacrifice all. "For God so loved the world that he gave his one and only Son, that whoever believes in him shall not perish but have eternal life."[225]

Doing evangelism isn't about what we can do and achieve; it's about what God has already done—through Jesus.

The Bible further tells us that God's love "has been poured out into our hearts through the Holy Spirit, who has been given to us." [226] It is this love that is our driving force when we share Jesus with others. As Paul writes, "For Christ's love compels us."[227]

I've met many Christians who get a guilty conscience when others talk about doing evangelism. They know that they should share the gospel with others. But inwardly they feel that doing evangelism is a heavy burden and a distasteful duty.

"If that's the way you feel about it," I always say, "then you shouldn't be sharing the gospel! Let somebody else take care of it!"

People tend to be surprised at my answer. Some even get provoked. "Don't you want people to hear the gospel? Don't you want people to get saved?"

Of course I do. But the Good News is *good news*. It's a message about God's love for us through Jesus Christ. It's important that the package matches the contents, and that the message bearer doesn't contradict the message. If we're driven by of a sense of duty or by a guilty conscience or a mix of both, we'll have a difficult time sharing God's love. Then we might as well leave it be.

The gospel is about God's love. Sara is driven neither out of sense of duty or from a bad conscience, but by the love that comes from God. God's love for the people at the retirement home is contagious through Sara. She doesn't just go around sharing the Good News; Sara goes around *being* the Good News.

M2-2-3 Carried by prayer

It is essential that evangelism be driven by God's love. But it is just as important that it is carried in prayer. All evangelism begins in prayer. As John Wesley once said, "All God's work is done through prayer."

"I urge, then, first of all, that petitions, prayers, intercession and thanksgiving be made for all people," writes Paul in his first letter to Timothy. In the same section he explains why prayer is so important: because God wants "all people to be saved and to come to a knowledge of the truth." [228]

When we pray, we make way for God, just as John the Baptist made way for Jesus. 'Prepare the way for the Lord, make straight paths for him. Every valley shall be filled in, every mountain and hill made low. The crooked roads shall become straight, the rough ways smooth. And all people will see God's salvation.' [229]

In the lives of those we pray for, there are high mountains, deep valleys, crooked roads, and rocky paths – things that keep them from seeing God's salvation. "Prepare the way for the Lord" is a commando shout to everyone who prays, and a strategy we can use in our prayer lives.

But how should we pray? It's not always easy to know: "We do not know what we ought to pray for."[230] Fortunately we have the Holy Spirit. He himself "intercedes for us through wordless groans."[231] He knows those we pray for. He knows the names of the high mountains and deep valleys in their lives; he knows where the roads are crooked and which paths are rocky.

The Holy Spirit knows these obstacles. We don't need to use our prayers to inform him of what he should do in a person's life. Instead, we can let the Holy Spirit inform us. Then we might find ourselves becoming the answer to our prayers. When you pray for neighbors, co-workers and classmates, you better be prepared for God to come and point at you and say, "I'm going to bless these people through *you!*"

Because of this, we should always add at the end of our prayers, "Here am I, Lord! Send me!"

[228] 1 Timothy 2:1-4

[229] Luke 3:4-6

[230] Romans 8:26

[231] Romans 8:26

232 Luke 19:10

233 John 15:5

234 1 John 1:1

235 Romans 5:5

236 John 3:16

M2-2-4 Close to Jesus – close to people

Evangelism can quickly become just another activity in the church, just like any other. For me, evangelism is a life and a lifestyle. Evangelism is about loving Jesus and giving practical expression to that love by being obedient to him and doing what he asks me to do.

"For the Son of Man came to seek and to save the lost," [232] said Jesus after he saved the life of Zacchaeus the tax collector. When we follow Jesus, he will lead us to the lost so that he, not us, can save them.

But this requires that we live so close to Jesus that we can hear his voice and follow him. "If you remain in me and I in you, you will bear much fruit; apart from me you can do nothing," [233] says Jesus.

The first disciples had a fresh revelation of Jesus: "That which was from the beginning, which we have heard, which we have seen with our eyes, which we have looked at and our hands have touched—this we proclaim concerning the Word of life." [234]

Two thousand years later, we can also have a fresh revelation of Jesus, because "God's love has been poured out into our hearts through the Holy Spirit, who has been given to us." [235] Let this love lead you to others. It is greater than the fear of man and concern about what others might say. The love that God has poured out into our hearts is the same love that caused God to send his only-begotten Son so that "whoever believes in him shall not perish but have eternal life."[236]

M2-3

THE HARVEST IS RIPE - BY ARNE SKAGEN

M2-3-1 Introduction

I had been invited by a church to hold a seminar on doing evangelism. It was a large church with several hundred members. But it was also a discouraged church. One after another, the people at the seminar stood up to witness to how little openness there was in the city to the gospel, and how uninterested people seemed to be. The church had tried to reach out to new people—really tried. There wasn't a lack of initiative and action. There had been a lot of work with little fruit, they told me. They hardly had seen one single person get saved the last years.

I listened to what they said. The discouragement seemed genuine. This was understandable after hearing the bad experiences they had gone through. After awhile I decided to ask the Holy Spirit how he looked at the situation in the city. Were things as stuck as they appeared? The Holy Spirit answered by filling me with expectancy and joy—expectancy that he really wanted to do something in the city and joy at the thought of the people who'll be experiencing God's love.

During a meeting at the church, I shared with them about the expectancy and joy I was feeling. I then mentioned a few names of people I believed the Holy Spirit had reminded me about (it happens now and then that He speaks to me in that way, by putting a name in my mind. The Spirit may speak to you in other ways, since He speaks to us in a thousand different ways).

I mentioned maybe ten to fifteen names in all. For each name I mentioned, there was someone in the audience who nodded in affirmation. "These people are the harvest," I said. "Let's pray for them."

After we had prayed, I encouraged those who knew these people to be bold the next days. "Share God's love in ways that feels natural to you." I also asked them to invite these people to attend a meeting or small group in the church.

Many said yes to the invitation (surprisingly many, thought those who did the inviting). A number of them received Jesus during the next days. There were even more who came later as we listened to the Holy Spirit and acted on his impulses.

237 Luke 10:2

M2-3-2 The harvest is plentiful

M2-3-2-1 What is a harvest?

"The harvest is plentiful," says Jesus. He doesn't bother to justify his statement. He just states what already is a fact. Nothing to discuss: the harvest *is* plentiful.

It is not the harvest Jesus intercedes for in Luke 10. Instead Jesus intercedes for the workers of the harvest, who are few. "Ask the Lord of the harvest, therefore, to send out workers into his harvest field."[237] "Plentiful harvest" means "many people". That is what I've always thought, anyway. But I think Jesus would like to say something *more* to us when he uses the expression "plentiful harvest." So it is important that we're able to grasp what he means.

What *is* a harvest? A harvest denotes a far advanced state, a late phase in a process. A seed is placed into the ground. It is nurtured by light and water. The seed has begun to sprout, and after a while it has made its way through the crust of the soil. Now it stands on the field as a mature ear of corn, ready to be gathered for the harvest – the seed has reached the condition of being ripe for the harvest. And so it works with people. They have come so far in their search for God that they appear as ripe harvest. They don't need any more evidence of God's existence. They don't need more leaflets stuck in their hands, no more invitations to church potluck dinners. They need someone to notice them, to take them seriously, and lead them through the last steps toward Jesus. When Jesus says that the harvest is plentiful, he means that many people are ready to receive him and his salvation.

M2-3-2-2 You are touching the harvest

You have probably heard the saying "You can't see the forest for the trees." I turn this around and say "We can't see the harvest for the people." This is our greatest challenge in the work of the harvest: Jesus says the harvest is plentiful, but it doesn't seem to catch our eye.

Our greatest challenge is the enemy's most important strategy. The enemy wants us to believe that the harvest is poor, and that this poor little harvest, with the greatest reluctance and with a whole lot of labor and toil, might let itself be harvested. And our own experience seems to confirm this: evangelism and harvesting is hard and complicated work associated with a lot of work and little fruit.

I believe Jesus wants to show us a way of working that gives less toil and more fruit. I once had a dream: I stood in the middle of a field, an enormous, vast field. It spread out in all directions, rolling, as far as the eye could see. Everywhere I turned I saw a ripe harvest: fat yellow ears of corn ready for the harvest. It was a spectacular view, and it filled me with excitement. But after a while the excitement turned into frustration. I stood in the middle of that enormous, yellow rectangle and looked desperately around. "Lord!" I cried, "Where should I start harvesting? Should I start over here? Or maybe it would be best to start on the other side – over there? How on earth should I approach this?"

The Lord of the harvest answered "Arne, look down." And then I noticed that the tip of my shoes touched some of ripe stalks of grain. The Lord of the harvest said, "*This* is where you begin. You can only harvest what you touch yourself."

The dream filled me with joy and peace (and that was my sign that it came from God). When I woke up the next morning I felt relieved. I realized that I didn't need to strive to find the harvest—I saw that I was surrounded by it.

I want to encourage you to pray that Jesus, the Lord of the harvest, will open your eyes. Let him take you and your Christian friends for a walk. Go together with Jesus through your neighborhood, your workplace, your circle of friends, and your family. Ask him to show you what's going on inside these people and what he's doing in their lives. Look, listen, and feel with all of your senses wide open. Let yourself be touched by what Jesus shows you. And if you don't experience anything at first, don't get discouraged. You are about to embark on a journey of discovery together with the Lord of the harvest. He is the Master; you are the disciple. He is the teacher; you are under training. Be patient and trusting, believe that the Teacher knows what he is doing.

"Come, follow me," Jesus said to the first disciples, "and I will send you out to fish for people."[238]

He says the same thing to you and me today. One of his first lessons is this: we are surrounded by a ripe harvest.

M2-3-2-3 The 4M syndrome

Jesus and his disciples are on their way from Jerusalem to Galilee. They take a shortcut through Samaria, an area many Jews walked around instead of through because of their hatred for the Samaritans.

[238] Matthew 4:19; Mark 1:17

[239] John 4:27-35

[240] 2 Corinthians 6:2

[241] John 4:39

When they arrive at Sychar, tired and hungry, the disciples disappear into the town to find some food. Jesus doesn't follow them; he sits by a well on the outskirts of town. And here he meets a woman who lives a sinful life. Jesus is aware of this, but he doesn't judge her. Instead he meets her with a love that makes her forget why she went to the well in the first place; she leaves her water jar behind and runs back to the town and tells everyone she meets: "Come, see a man who told me everything I ever did!" When the disciples find Jesus by the well, food is still the only thing they can think about: "Rabbi, eat something." Jesus replies rather briskly, "My food is to do the will of him who sent me and to finish his work." And then he corrects the disciples. "Don't you have a saying, 'It's still four months until harvest? I tell you, open your eyes and look at the fields! They are ripe for harvest."[239]

Many Christians today seem to have the same attitude as the disciples in Sychar: "Not today. But maybe great things will happen in about four months' time." I call this "The 4M Syndrome" (The Four Month Syndrome). It is widespread among God's people. We have a four-month buffer in our prayers and our expectations in God. He says: "Now is the time of God's favor, now is the day of salvation!"[240] But we say: "The right time will be in about four months; *then* the day of salvation will come!"

Those four extra months represent our lack of experience (or negative experience) with the harvest. By shoving all of our expectations into the future we shield ourselves from disappointment and failure today. The problem is that we also shield ourselves against the opportunities that God gives us right here, right now. We lose any expectation of people being saved today.

The woman at the well of Sychar was not affected by The 4M Syndrome; she didn't just sit down and wait for a suitable occasion to witness about Jesus. She instead left the water jar behind and went straight into town. It turned out to be full of people ripe for the harvest. "Many of the Samaritans from that town believed in him because of the woman's testimony...."[241]

Just minutes before this the disciples had also been to town. They could have shared even more about Jesus than what the Samarian woman could. But they didn't. The only thing that was on their minds was getting their own needs met: FOOD! NOW! When the disciples came into town they "couldn't see the harvest for the people." It was only after Jesus admonished them to lift up their eyes and *see* did they notice the harvest: all the people walking toward them on their way to meet Jesus, who had heard the testimony of a woman who had forgotten all about her own needs in her eagerness to tell others about Jesus.

[242] Matt 19:17

[243] Luke 19:1-10

M2-3-3 Understand the language of the harvest

M2-3-3-1 The example of Jesus

The harvest is ripe. Jesus has already established this. Now we'll see how the harvest has its own *language*. The harvest sends out *signals*; it *talks*. If we can learn to recognize the language of the harvest when we hear it, I am convinced that we, both as individuals and as churches, will experience a breakthrough in people's acceptance of Jesus.

Jesus understood the language of the harvest better then anyone else. His ear for the language was so finely tuned that he could perceive the difference between the genuine language and the not-so-genuine varieties of the harvest language.

Picture a rich, young man who comes to you and asks: "What good thing can I do to have eternal life?" What would you have thought? I know what I would have thought: "Language of the harvest! Ripe ears of corn! Pass me the sickle!"

A rich, young man came to Jesus and asked exactly this question. Jesus answered him by asking a question in return: "Why do you ask me about what is good? There is only One who is good. If you want to enter life, keep the commandments."[242]

As the conversation evolves, it becomes clear that the rich young man was a seeker only up to a certain point: his money. When Jesus puts his finger on this area, the man walks away in distress. He appeared to be ripe for the harvest, but in reality he wasn't.

Zacchaeus was also wealthy—very wealthy. As the chief tax collector in the service of the occupying powers, he had gotten wealthy at the cost of his fellow citizens. In contrast to the rich young man, there was nothing about Zacchaeus that suggests that he is ripe for the harvest. He placed himself at the outer edge, so to speak, of the day's events when Jesus visited Jericho. At a distance, from his green, little branch, he watched the commotion around the carpenter's son from Nazareth.[243]

[244] Luke 19:6

[245] Luke 10:5-6

[246] 1 Timothy 2:1

Who knows what goes on behind a man's more-or-less pious façade? We're often wrong when it comes to this. We stare ourselves blind by looking at the exterior and jump to hasty conclusions. Jesus doesn't do this. He looks past the exterior, observing what's happening on the inside. This day in Jericho he lifts his eyes over the crowd and sees the harvest in a sycamore-fig tree. What is it that makes Zacchaeus forget his rich-man-dignity and, just like a kid, climb up a tree?

The language of the body can also be the language of the harvest. With his short little body up in a tree, Zacchaeus says without saying a word: "Look at me! Look at my loneliness, my longing, my sense of loss." In places like well-to-do Norway where I live, I believe we are surrounded by Zacchaeuses. But do we see them? Do we recognize the discreet signals they're sending out? Do we hear the subtle language of the harvest?

M2-3-3-2   Someone who promotes peace

When Jesus asks Zacchaeus to come down from the tree, this is how Luke describes his reaction: "So he came down at once and welcomed him gladly."[244]

This is the way someone who *promotes peace* reacts. She receives Jesus with joy. She listens to what Jesus has to say. She accepts the new life Jesus wants to give. We are not called to shake people down from the trees against their will; we are called to go to those who are already longing for Jesus, people who may not even be aware of their longing.

In Luke 10 Jesus sends out the disciples "to every town and place where he was about to go." Before sending the disciples two by two, he gives them clear instructions about who they should spend time on:

> "When you enter a house, first say, 'Peace to this house." If someone who promotes peace is there, your peace will rest in them; if not, it will return to you."[245]

As disciples of Jesus we carry out "intercession and thanksgiving for all people."[246] But the ones we are to spend most of our time with are those that Jesus calls "someone who promotes peace." These are people who greet us openly with friendliness. They listen to what we have to say, ask questions, and give response. These are the people Jesus asks us to spend most of our time with, not those who are only looking for a debate and to win an argument.

There are many people who promote peace—the place is swarming with them! I can guarantee you that you have them in your own network—in your family, neighborhood, and workplace. And the exciting part is that "people who promote peace" usually know other "people who promote peace," which is how the network grows.

Find a sheet of paper and a pen. Write your name on the paper and draw a circle around it. Outside of the circle you draw new circles.

Sit quietly back. Ask the Holy Spirit to take you on a journey through your network; from the people you know well to your more peripheral acquaintances. Ask the Holy Spirit to tell you what he sees, what is going on in your network. Listen to the Spirit and talk with him about what he shows you. Write down in one of the empty circles whenever a name comes to your mind.

Do you *see*? People who promote peace already exist in your network. You are surrounded by the harvest. And what you have written so far is only *your* network. Imagine if everyone in your church or house group sat down and drew a similar network map! Then we would catch a glimpse of a much greater harvest. We could then look closer at how we can *stand together* in the work of the harvest and touch *each other's* networks. But more about this in the next section "Together in the harvest."

M2-3-4 Together in the harvest

M2-3-4-1 Not alone

Harvesting is teamwork; it's not a solo game. This is one of the most important lessons I've learned as a worker in the harvest in the kingdom of God.

For a long time I was convinced that it was just the opposite. I was only concerned about *my ministry and what I could do on my own. Fortunately the Lord has – with a great deal of help from my Christian brothers and sisters – saved me from my own self-sufficiency. I realized that we achieve much more by working together, shoulder-to-shoulder on a work team. And this is the way the Bible recommends to do it, anyway.*

"If they were all one part, where would the body be? As it is, there are many parts, but one body. The eye cannot say to the hand, "I don't need you!" And the

247 1 Corinthians
12:19-21

head cannot say to the feet, "I don't need you!" Quite the opposite! The parts of the body that may seem weakest are precisely the ones that are necessary… Now, you are the body of Christ, and each one of you is a part of it."[247]

When we work together to win each other's family, friends and neighbors, we can help each other by doing what we do best, what we are gifted to do. Who is doing what is not important. The important thing is that everyone does what God has asked him or her to do. Some are good at noticing and including people. Others have a special ability to meet specific needs. Some are good at starting conversations and asking just the right questions. And then there are those who've received a special gift to lead people through last steps to Jesus.

I have seen this interaction unfold time and time again, such as in a house church or a cell group. It is just as fascinating every time it happens: someone has invited a neighbor, a colleague, or a friend to the Christian fellowship. In the beginning he might be reserved and questioning: What has he gotten himself into? But then, in a cozy atmosphere filled with the presence of God, he starts to relax a bit. From one person in the group he receives some encouragement, from a second person a word of knowledge, from a third person a nice hot cup of coffee, while a fourth prays for one of his concrete needs. This is the way Jesus uses the Christian fellowship – through the parts, the *participant's different personalities and gifts – to touch someone with his love.*

M2-3-4-2 It all started on the ferry

John is sitting on a ferry on his way to an island on the west coast of Norway. A group of friends sits down at the next table; their conversation becomes loud and intense. it's not very difficult to discern what they're talking about since "God" and "Jesus" are mentioned in every other sentence.

John becomes curious, so he discreetly moves a bit closer. In the beginning nobody notices him, but then they discover that they have an eavesdropper. One of them turns to the man and greets him. At first he's a little awkward, but soon he is dragged into the conversation and a nice chat ensues. As the ferry docks, they ask the man if he'd like to come to a meeting that evening in the home of some Christians living on the island.

John is busy that night, but a week later he shows up. He is well received by the others, and the openness and warmth from the others does something to him. When he returns the week after, he has a buddy with him, Tom.

At this meeting, John is challenged to accept Jesus. The idea is not new to John; he's already thought about that many times. He answers with a crooked smile: "I'll wait until Monday. I've planned to go to a party and get drunk this weekend – one last time." "Sure, that's up to you," says Jim, one of the leaders of the community, adding, "If that's what you really want." This comment starts a conversation between the two of them. John starts to reflect upon what he *really wants*. In the end, he sees no good reason to postpone it any longer, and that same evening he invites Jesus into his life.

His buddy Tom is witness to John's decision. Soon after he chooses to do the same.

M2-3-4-3 Mapping-out the networks

Through the years I've been allowed to help churches with their harvest work. The churches, no matter how different they've been from each other, have had one thing in common: When they start to look closer at their social networks, new doors open in all directions. The process of identifying social networks is an eye-opener, for both the members and the leaders of the church.

When we help a church to reach people, we start by asking people in the church: Who is in your network? Who do you experience as being positive towards you? Who listens when you share your faith, and who asks inquisitive questions? Who knocks on your door when they need help with a practical matter; who comes to you with their personal problems? In other words – or in the words of Jesus in Luke 10: Who promotes peace in your network?

In this mapping phase we are dependent on asking the Holy Spirit for guidance and advice. He knows your network much better than you do. He knows what's going on inside your contacts, who's the most open to Jesus. If you let the Holy Spirit show you this, you will often be surprised: He might draw your attention to someone else than you first thought! After the members of the church have done some thinking, and the Holy Spirit has done some speaking, we ask them to take a piece of paper and draw their network.

When you then place your drawing next to someone else's, you soon discover something exciting: there are points of contact between the networks! Some of the names in your network are also on the other drawings. Finally we can work on the same case. We can pray for each other's contacts and make creative

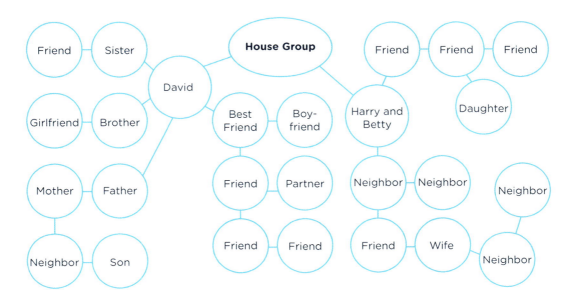

plans on how to reach into and touch each other's networks. This sounds great, doesn't it?

On paper, sure, but in the real world – does it work?

M2-3-4-4 Example: Leicester, England

In Leicester, England, there is a church of about 250 active members. The church has had an even, but not very strong, growth over many years.

In 2007 the church started to focus on harvest work in the city. The members came together to practice sharing the gospel about Jesus as well as giving their personal testimonies. They received teaching on how to recognize the voice of the Spirit, and how to pray for people. During the meetings in the church, a great deal of time was given to the testimonies of people who had shared the gospel with someone before, or who prayed for the sick.

My task was to help identify the social networks of the people in the church. I asked them "Who do you feel the Holy Spirit speaks to you about among your acquaintances? Do you know someone who could use a touch of God's power?"

Many other questions were asked to help people open their eyes to the harvest lying and waiting. People were encouraged to be creative, and to ask God to show them new ways of making contact with people. Since people are so different, we need different meeting points to touch them. We spoke a lot about how the Holy Spirit probably wouldn't "blow" the harvest into the church building all by himself! We saw that it was more likely that the Spirit would "blow" the people of the church out of the building – and towards the waiting harvest.

In June 2008, we planned a week where the members would move towards people they felt God had reminded them of during the mapping phase. People took up the challenge. They called friends and neighbors; they invited them over for breakfast, lunch, dinner, afternoon tea, and a late evening meal. There were barbeque parties, cheese parties and other parties. The members of the church got involved in each other's networks, and used each other's equipping and gifts across the different networks. This turned out to be a catalyst for what happened next.

During the following three weeks the church saw four, five people accept Jesus *every day.* Some were healed from cancer and other diseases and others were set free from drug addiction. Before June was up a lot of people in the church got to see their friends, neighbors, and work colleagues be born again – people they had long prayed for without ever realizing that they were ripe for the harvest.

Some started working with immigrants and asylum seekers. They gave practical help to their new fellow citizens in their daily lives—helped them to fill out forms for official documents and to improve their English. Every week they had their own meetings, where many received Jesus. The key was the practical care and the love they experienced from people in the church.

So, moving on to the critical question: Are all who received Jesus in June 2008 attending the church today? I wish I could answer yes, but with hand over my heart, I honestly cannot. Just *three out of four are* still active members of the church! What made three-quarters of them stay in most cases was that they already had a relationship with someone in the church—and these relationships only tend to strengthen after they've become Christians. Discipling the new Christians starts from Day One (actually earlier: from the day someone in the church started to pray for them). The fact that Jesus wants to be Lord of each person's life is made clear from the very beginning; it doesn't come as a bombshell two years after conversion.

Does the church in Leicester still experience the same sort of growth today? Not quite; but they still see people get saved every week. As they say, "There's been a paradigm shift. We've started to think and act differently."

It all started with the church taking seriously Jesus' instructions in Luke 10. By focusing on the people who promote peace, they got in touch with those who Jesus "himself had planned to visit." Jesus planned to visit them, but he sent the people of the church ahead of him. And then he came, bringing salvation, restoration and new life.

As I've been known to say on occasion: "Let's go – he'll be coming soon!"

M2-4

"I HAVE FULLY PROCLAIMED THE GOSPEL" – BY ARNT JAKOB HOLVIK

[248] Romans 15:18-19

M2-4-1 Introduction

Church planting is about making new disciples. That is the mission Jesus gave us. According to the Bible, if we want to make new disciples for Jesus, we have to preach the gospel. Paul, who is the church planter prototype, sums up his apostolic service like this:

> "I will not venture to speak of anything except what Christ has accomplished through me in leading the Gentiles to obey God by what I have said and done – by the power of signs and wonders, through the power of the Spirit of God. So from Jerusalem all the way around Illyricum, I have fully proclaimed the gospel of Christ." [248]

We can draw four main points out of this scripture:

1. First, Paul states that Christ has worked through him during his service. The grace of God – *Christ at work* – is the reason Paul was able to lead the Gentiles to obedience. When God uses us to lead people to salvation, or when wonders and healings happen through our hands, we must not take the glory ourselves, for it is God's work. Christ works through us, so *he* should get the glory. This is absolutely essential. Guard your heart and give the glory to God!

2. Second, Paul states that he led the Gentiles to obedience under Jesus' Lordship through what he said, and that he has fully proclaimed the gospel of Christ "all the way around".

3. Third, he led the Gentiles to obedience through what he had "said and done." We can associate acts of love and compassion to what is "done". This is an important aspect of service to God in both the Old and New Testaments. Here we will relate this theme to the church-planting context.

4. Fourth, Paul states that it was his preaching, accompanied by the power of signs and wonders through the power of the Spirit of God, which led

the Gentiles to obey God. There is a clear element of God's power in his apostolic service.

Central to Paul's international church-planting ministry was preaching the gospel in the power dimension of the kingdom of God. When we realize from the New Testament that this was central in Jesus' earthly ministry and in the ministry of the other apostles, there is every reason to believe that we need this in our church-planting ministries as well! This can only happen if God works through us, but this is exactly what he wants to do! And if the love of God can be expressed through our lives, we have all reason to believe that the Word of God will advance and that many churches will be planted through our service for God!

M2-4-2 The Gospel – "The power of God that brings salvation"

Let's first look at the *good news* Jesus sent us to proclaim.

M2-4-2-1 Good news!

The Greek word *"Evangelion"* means "good message" or "good news". We are actually sent out to preach *good* news to people, not *bad* news! Jesus proclaimed the good news of God's kingdom right from the start:

> "After John was put in prison, Jesus went to Galilee, proclaiming the good news of God. 'The time has come,' he said. 'The kingdom of God has come near. Repent and believe the good news!'"[249]

The beginning of the coming of God's kingdom was when Jesus Christ came, lived, served, and died for the sins of the whole world, took our punishment, defeated the devil, sin and death; was raised up to new life in the resurrection, went up to Heaven and sent the Holy Spirit! After that the disciples are the witnesses and preachers of God's kingdom, salvation, and eternal life in Jesus Christ! Now we are the ones to tell people from all the nations about the lordship of Jesus Christ and make them his disciples.

[250] Romans 1:16-17

M2-4-2-2 The Power of God that brings salvation lies within the Word

It is absolutely essential to understand that the Word of God, the good news, holds *within itself* the power to give new life! The gospel *is* the power of God that brings salvation. Paul proclaims:

> "For I am not ashamed of the gospel, because it is the power of God that brings salvation to everyone who believes: first to the Jew, then to the Gentile. For in the gospel the righteousness of God is revealed – a righteousness that is by faith from first to last, just as it is written: "The righteous will live by faith."[250]

This is made clear in Jesus' teaching of the sower. In the parable of the sower and the seed, it is the seed, the word of the kingdom, which *in itself* has the power to bring new life and growth. The power to bring salvation to man is inherent in the Word. A consequence of this is that if we don't preach the gospel of Jesus Christ and the kingdom of God to unbelievers, basically no one can be saved! And so it is imperative that church planters preach the gospel of Jesus Christ to those who do not have him as their Lord.

In many churches we find a tendency to sit and wait for people to be saved. We even pray for this to happen, and truly hope that it will. Yet very little seems to happen. But how can they be saved if we don't go out and preach to them? Keep this in mind as you do church planting!

Imagine two farmers who want a crop to grow in their fields. They both make sure that fertilizer is spread and that the land is plowed. They also make sure that there's enough water. Then one farmer sows seed, but the other doesn't sow anything. After awhile a huge crop grows all on its own in the field of the first farmer. The farmer is delighted! But the second farmer just doesn't understand: Why didn't *he* get any crops?

Sometimes we think that people will be saved if we just arrange meetings and different activities in the church. Or we think people will come to faith by us living respectable and decent lives. We *must* share the gospel of Jesus Christ, because faith comes from *preaching*! Paul says:

[251] Romans 10:14-15

[252] Romans 10:9

"How, then, can they call on the one they have not believed in? And how can they believe in the one of whom they have not heard? And how can they hear without someone preaching to them? And how can anyone preach unless they are sent? As it is written: 'How beautiful are feet of those who bring good news!'"[251]

We are the ones who are sent to preach the good news! Therefore, sow abundantly. Then you can receive a huge crop of new believers, with new churches following after. Do what Jesus and the apostles did in their church-planting work: Preach the gospel and make disciples!

M2-4-2-3 Harvesting people

We need to harvest people and teach them to keep all that Jesus has commanded. There comes a time in when people are ready to repent and make the decision to follow Jesus. But people don't necessarily come running to us to tell us that this what they want to do. It is important, therefore, that we are awake and ready to listen to the guidance of the Spirit for the right timing to challenge and invite people to repent and start a new life with Jesus as Lord.

"If you declare with your mouth, 'Jesus is Lord,' and believe in your heart that God raised him from the dead, you will be saved."[252]

In my work on the west coast of Norway, I've experienced how preaching the gospel of Jesus Christ and the kingdom of God has changed many lives. For example, sometimes I've experienced that people suddenly understand the gospel when I tell them about it. They might have heard something about Jesus before, but they never fully understood what he did here on earth or why this concerns them. The death and resurrection of Jesus remains an historical event they don't grasp the meaning of and which they only partly believe in. But when I, by faith, have explained to them the core of the gospel in a simple way, I experience how they suddenly understand and grasp the message with their heart. When you share the message with someone in this way, you allow the Holy Spirit to reveal it to them and convince them that they need Jesus and salvation in their own life. Preaching is a central part of the mission Jesus gave us as his disciples.

[253] Matthew 28:18-20

[254] Luke 19:10

[255] Acts 10:38

M2-4-3 The commission and the mission

The mission from Jesus goes like this:

> "All authority in heaven and on earth has been given to me. Therefore go and make disciples of all nations, baptizing them in the name of the Father and of the Son and of the Holy Spirit, and teaching them to obey everything I have commanded you. And surely I am with you always, to the very end of the age."[253]

This sending is also for us today. We are called to go out and make disciples of all nations, so both Jews and Gentiles can come to faith in Jesus Christ, the Messiah, before he returns like he he said he would.

M2-4-3-1 Biblical line of mission

The Bible clarifies how the missional sending begins with God himself: the Father sent Jesus, the Word, from Heaven down to the darkness on earth. Jesus said about himself and his mission: "For the Son of Man came to seek and to save the lost."[254] *He went from place to place and town to town and preached the good news, healed the sick, drove out demons, forgave sin, etc. In the Book of Acts the ministry of Jesus is summed up like this:*

> "God anointed Jesus of Nazareth with the Holy Spirit and power, and he went around doing good and healing all who were under the power of the devil, because God was with him."[255]

And so Jesus sent the disciples two by two to do the same, first the twelve, and then the 72. After Jesus died on the cross and was raised from the dead, he gave the disciples instructions to wait in Jerusalem for what the Father had promised – power from on high. And he sent them out to the nations through the Great Commission.

256 1 Corinthians 4:20

The first thing that happened when the Holy Spirit was sent from heaven to the disciples was that they started to preach about God in many languages. The gospel broke the barriers of language with the help of the Holy Spirit. After some time, Stephen was stoned to death, and a great persecution hit the church of Jerusalem to the point where all apart from the apostles were scattered. Acts 8:4 says, "Those who had been scattered preached the word wherever they went." The Gospel was even preached in Samaria to the Ethiopian eunuch.

And then a revelation came to Peter about the clean and unclean, which was immediately followed by the event that happened in Cornelius' house where the Holy Spirit came upon the Gentiles! Again, the work of the Holy Spirit, God himself, broke the borders for preaching the gospel. Not only would the Jews hear the gospel, but the Gentiles as well. After that, the apostles went to other countries and preached, just like Paul, until the gospel eventually reached the European continent. Church history claims that some of the original apostles also preached in many different countries in other areas of the world.

Still today, more than 2000 years later, the gospel of God's kingdom and Jesus Christ is preached all around the globe, because of the Great Commission Jesus gave. And the Spirit is continuously working to bring the testimony of Jesus to unreached people and people groups. This will go on until every nation has been reached with the gospel.

What we are seeing is a missional movement that started *with God himself,* who through Jesus Christ and the Holy Spirit brings the good news of the kingdom and salvation to the people and nations of the world. This is not a mission for a chosen few, but it is God's own mission, his love and plan of salvation, which is preached today through the body of Christ – the Church – which is us. Mission is fundamental to the life and ministry of the church—not just for a select group of especially interested or extraordinarily gifted people. *Together* we are sent to preach the gospel to the world!

M2-4-4 The power dimension

M2-4-4-1 The kingdom of God is of power

It is essential that we understand Paul's statement: "For the kingdom of God is not a matter of talk but of power."[256] Here we speak of an *invisible* spiritual kingdom of power that has *visible* consequences. The Word of God further tells us: "…and you will see the Son of man sitting at the right hand of the Mighty One and coming on the clouds of heaven."[257] One of God's names revealed in Scripture is "the Mighty One."

With this perspective we should mention that is was *the power of God* that raised Jesus from the dead. The Resurrection is at the core of the plan of salvation. This power also works also in us who believe, and one day it will raise us up to eternal life.[258]

The truth is that God's kingdom is a kingdom of power, and we need God's power if we are to be living witnesses of the resurrection of Jesus. We see it manifested on Pentecost: It wasn't until the Holy Spirit – the "power from on high"—came over the believers that they were ready to be Jesus' witnesses to the nations; they got the courage to preach from the fire that came upon them. It was this that Jesus was referring to when he spoke earlier of the baptism of the Holy Spirit.[259]

M2-4-4-2 An historical example from Norway: Hans Nielsen Hauge

In 1796 Hans Nielsen Hauge, the twenty-five year old son of a Norwegian farmer, had a powerful encounter with the Spirit and love of God. Soon after people he met started to repent and turn to God. Hauge preached in the power of the Spirit as he travelled around Norway to establish a number of businesses. This was the start of a powerful awakening that came to deeply impact the nation, and which today—more than 200 years later—characterizes Norway as a nation. One of the foundation stones of the awakening was the house church movement that emerged in Hauge's footprints. People met in homes to study and hear the word of God and to seek God in prayer. The movement of "The Haugians" would eventually influence Norway at all levels of society, from the grassroots level, in business life and trade, through the printing of books, and all the way to the Parliament. The Spirit and power of God was active, and Norway as a nation is still influenced today by what happened at that time.

M2-4-4-3 Visible results of power in ministry

When Jesus sent the twelve apostles, he *"gave them authority to drive out impure spirits and to heal every disease and sickness"*[260] and further: *"Go, proclaim this message: 'The kingdom of heaven has come near.' Heal the sick, raise the dead, cleanse those who have leprosy, drive out demons. Freely you have received; freely give."*[261]

[257] Mark 14:62

[258] 1 Corinthians 6:14

[259] Acts 1:4-5

[260] Matthew 10:1

[261] Matthew 10:7-8

Mark 16:15-18 I believe that God often equips people with his power in a special way when they're to go out in missions or in an apostolic pioneer ministry. One reason why we particularly need God's power in these situations is that we bring the kingdom of God to dark places where spiritual powers have influence and where many people live far from God. They need to be saved and discipled. They need to be baptized in water and filled with the Holy Spirit into a new life!

This is what I experience in my own ministry. But such things as spiritual authority and physical healing aren't given to us so that we can immaturely brag about it afterward, as if the glory goes to us. The power of God is absolutely necessary for us as we minister to people living in darkness without hope. They need a new life, and so God has to step in. You and I are dependent on the power of God in our ministry so that the salvation and kingdom of God can break through to unreached lives and places.

M2-4-4-4 For all who believe

In the Great Commission in the gospel of Mark, Jesus says:

> "Go into all the world and preach the gospel to all creation. Whoever believes and is baptized will be saved, but whoever does not believe will be condemned. And these signs will accompany those who believe: In my name they will drive out demons; they will speak in new tongues; they will pick up snakes with their hands; and when they drink deadly poison, it will not hurt them at all; they will place their hands on sick people, and they will get well."[262]

This is for all "those who believe." It is interesting to note that Jesus, Peter and Paul saw healings, deliverance from demons, and signs and wonders happen all the time in their ministries. If you read the gospels and the Book of Acts, a relatively high percentage of the verses are about these things. So we can conclude that this must have been important to God and it must have been an integral part of the coming of the kingdom of God, through the Son of God and his apostles. Paul's teaching of the spiritual gifts – and their widespread use in the early church – show us that these factors were well known and happened as part of the coming of the kingdom of God and the ministry of the Church in the *world. Therefore – have faith in God and dare to enter these fields in your own ministry.*

[263] Psalm 103:3

[264] Isaiah 53:4-5

M2-4-4-5 God's loving intervention

When Jesus told us to "place your hands on sick people, and they will get well," the background for this is in who God is and in the ministry of Jesus. In the Psalms David says about God: "He forgives all your sins and heals all your diseases."[263] *In Isaiah we find a prophecy of Jesus:*

> "Surely he took up our pain and bore our suffering, yet we considered him punished by God, stricken by him, and afflicted. But he was pierced for our iniquities; the punishment that brought us peace was on him, and by his wounds we are healed."[264]

The words from Isaiah about healing are repeated in Jesus' ministry in Matthew 8:17 in the New Testament. God is a God who heals and forgives. This is his very nature, and he has done this through his work of salvation. We know that God sent Jesus Christ because he loves us so. For the same reason he heals and drives out demons. A sick person suffering from illness, and a person plagued by demons live in a terrible captivity. In his love God intervenes, because he loves them. Not only does he forgive sin, he also heals and provides freedom from demons.

M2-4-4-6 The power of God builds faith in people's lives

In the place where I now live, we've seen people come to faith in Jesus Christ through healings and wonders. For example, people have come to faith after being healed from serious damage to their backs, serious bone fractures, paralysis, and after being set free from reading and learning disabilities, depressions, and suicidal thoughts. When we've been out traveling, we've also witnessed the lame walk, the blind see, the deaf hear, and people set free from demons. This is the way God touches people's lives, and it can lead them to faith in the message.

M2-4-4-7 Already – but not yet

The coming of God's kingdom will not be complete until Jesus returns to earth. Then he will establish his eternal and perfect kingdom, and evil will receive its verdict. Before this happens, however, we must live in tension between a fallen world and the kingdom of God that goes forth like a small mustard seed sown in the ground and to become a plant that grows bigger and bigger. It is because of this that we experience both victory and pain in this life. The gospels clearly speak of the pain that is a part of following Jesus, specifically about the persecution that comes because of the gospel.

The pain and guilt of the human race is a consequence of the fall, and we all face this in our lives. We all need grace, encouragement, and comfort from both God and from each other. At the same time God intervenes in the world by letting his kingdom come. It is a kingdom that is made visible through love, grace, forgiveness, joy, good deeds, and justice. It is also a kingdom where healing, freedom, and wonders happen. Therefore we boldly go with the gospel of salvation and love to people who live separated from God in darkness, knowing that God goes with us, confirming the message through signs and wonders.

M2-4-5 Practical love – diaconal service

In Acts Chapter Six we hear of a new ministry in the church: *bread distribution*. Providing practical help for the poor, widows, and orphans is also seen in the Old Testament. It is interesting to read in the Word how deacons were appointed to lead this ministry. This was apparently an important service for the church in Jerusalem.

The diaconal ministry is something we should bring with us into the work of church planting. When we plant a church, we not only plant the gospel among people who don't know Jesus—we also plant our own lives. The incarnational Jesus came and made his dwelling among us; in the same way we need to plant our own lives in love among those God loves.

In the history of the Church, there are many examples of how the poor and suffering were ministered to and loved, a type of incarnation of God's love through the body of Christ. A recent and very famous example of this is Mother Teresa's work among the poor, dying and destitute in the slums of Calcutta, India. She, along with the sisters who served with her and still serve after Mother Teresa's death, committed herself to a life of poverty, chastity, and service for the poor with a love that is difficult to express in words. The love and grace of God in her work has had ripple effects over the entire world, and Mother Teresa's life stands as a testimony to the love of Jesus for the poor. Her life is also a testimony to what is possible when the love of God drives a person to a holy life in service to those whom Jesus gave his life for.

[265] Matthew 25:40

Mother Teresa had the perspective of Jesus in her service to the poor and suffering. Jesus says: "Whatever you did for one of the least of these brothers and sisters of mine, you did for me."[265] Here he speaks of the hungry, the thirsty, the naked, the sick, and the imprisoned. They need our love and care. When Mother Teresa served and loved them, she was serving Jesus.

M2-4-6 Preaching and power

M2-4-6-1 The way to reach people through the church planting team
When you are planting a church it is important to ask yourself:

» Are we preaching the gospel to non-Christians? If yes, who?

» How many non-Christians do we meet in the course of a week, and in which arenas do we meet them?

» Are we conscious of—and have a strategy for—where, when, and how we can meet non-Christians and share the gospel with them on a regular basis?

These questions are worth asking. Having a strategy for how you can reach people doesn't make your ministry something mechanical or artificial. If the Holy Spirit is the driving force in your ministry, then your Spirit-led strategies can be seen as an expression of God's love.

M2-4-6-2 For the mouth speaks of what flows from the heart
It takes being filled with the Holy Spirit for a person to bring people to Jesus. Therefore living close to God may be the most important thing we can do in a church-planting work. We can become so busy in our church-planting ministry that our own relationship with God can suffer for it. We can also end up being driven by the wrong motives.

If you are driven in your ministry by the selfish ambition of success and results measured in numbers, your true spiritual life starts to die as the flesh takes over. You work hard, but with less and less joy. Gradually you start building your own kingdom rather than being part of building God's. You boldly share testimonies you know by heart, but your own life is about to run dry. If this starts happening, it's time to repent!

For from the abundance of the heart the mouth speaks. We need to be filled with the Holy Spirit and his love. Then things turn out all right, both in our own lives and in our church-planting ministry.

M2-4-6-3 Witnessing in our daily lives

For members of the church planting team who have regular work, the workplace is a natural arena to share the gospel. You witness by living your life with integrity and character, by doing an honest and decent job and by showing care for your colleagues. Be strong and courageous in sharing the gospel and the things God has done in your life! Personal testimonies communicate well. Praying for people's needs at the workplace is another good way to lead people into an encounter with God. When God enters into their situation as an answer to prayer, you can tell them more and help them to get to know God through Jesus Christ.

It can be quite demanding for some to be the only Christian at work. Having your church planting teammates as a source of encouragement and strength can help you go to work revived and filled with the Holy Spirit!

M2-4-6-4 Strategic planning

It is wise to be strategic in church planting. Pray and ask God to guide you as to which group or groups of people your team is meant to reach out to and focus on. Pray about, reflect on, and identify the arenas where you can meet these people. Examples of such arenas are youth centers, existing social networks, a café, the streets, organized leisure activities, or the neighborhood. The team can also create their own arenas, such as arranging an international lunch for immigrants, holding an Alpha Course and creating activities for children in the neighborhood. There are many opportunities to meet people and build relationships with them.

M2-4-6-5 Power evangelism

When it comes to healing by the power of the Spirit, we need to act on the Word of God. If we believe in his Word, we will also do what it tells us to do. This is the case with healing: Place your hands on the sick and they will be healed, says

Jesus. So you should just do this on your team. People come with many needs; there are those who are sick or injured, and some who have mental health issues such as depression or anxiety. Even though things can be complicated and complex, we can always pray. If you start to step out in faith in these matters, you will see God show up.

People's need for healing and freedom from distress can come to your attention through a conversation during lunch at work, or on the bus, during a house visit or at a party—or at an intercession stand you set up in the city square where you live. Needs become known whenever you meet with people. If you want to, you can just ask someone: "Are you sick or injured? Do you need healing for anything?" It doesn't have to be more complicated than that. If the person you're talking to wants prayer and you lay your hands on them to pray for healing, remember to ask if he or she had experienced any change. If the person uses crutches, ask if he or she can try to walk. Expect God's intervention!

M2-4-6-6 Acts of mercy
Within diaconal work there are many people in every society who need love and care. Wherever you are, there are people who are poor, have drug or alcohol addictions, who are hurt from a broken relationship or divorce, are sick, lonely, mentally ill or unemployed, children who are neglected by their parents, refugees and immigrants and so on.

In addition to being there for people as a good neighbor, your church planting team can take the initiative to set up ministries such as a home-visiting service, volunteer center, Christian youth café, a counseling center for married couples and families with difficulties and for teenage pregnancy counseling. There are many possibilities. In the early stages of a church-planting work, there is a limit as to what your team actually has the capacity to do; so you need to be sensitive to the Spirit's guidance and to the specific needs of the community—as well as to the type of people and gifts you have on your team.

No matter the situation, it is the love of God that touches people through our lives. Every person is valuable to God, and this is how the kingdom of God expands—one person at a time, changed by Jesus Christ until the nations have become his disciples!

M 2 - 5

FROM WORD TO ACTION

We believe that what we have written below is one of the most important sections of this book. You will find questions and exercises both for the individual and for those of you who are working as a team. We have also included various case studies for each of the main themes of the book. At the end of the book you'll find a checklist for each of the exercises, as well as the learning goals we've had for each of the themes. If you wish to learn more, you can read through the suggested literature list to see if you'd like to order a book for further reading.

The individual exercises, Team exercises and case studies are specifically geared for each of the secondary themes of the book. These can be used to generate discussion during team meetings. When used this way, it will be important that each team member goes through the material to prepare him or herself ahead of time.

The checklist and learning goals are found at the very end of this section. When you go through them, you can chart your own progress: Are we doing what's been suggested, or is it just more head-knowledge? Are we working in the intended direction of the chapter? In this way you'll be able to measure your progress against the learning goals for each chapter.

M2-5-1   For chapter M2-1: Pioneer work and comfort zones – by Øystein Gjerme

M2-5-1-1   Team exercise 1:
Do an analysis on the various religious options available in the culture or region you'll be doing church planting in. How do you believe that these options might affect people's perceptions of your team's initiative?

M2-5-1-2   Team exercise 2:
Make a list of seven to ten questions that would be relevant in forming a picture of the culture your team will be doing church planting in. Do interviews, gather facts and figures, and collect news clips and magazine articles to help find answers to your questions. Draw a sketch or diagram that gives a visual picture of the context in which you'll be doing church planting.

M2-5-1-3 Team exercise 3:

In light of the material you have gathered on the cultural context your team will be working in, solidify which choices and priorities you must make in order to reach your intended group.

M2-5-1-4 Individual exercises

Read Acts 10:9-16 and reflect on your own religious stereotypes and perceptions that may be challenged when you meet people who don't know God. Make a list of these. How do you believe God will need to change *you* in order for you to reach these people?

M2-5-1-5 Case study 1

Hannah and Joe lead a church planting team consisting of themselves, four families and six students. They plan to plant a church and bring the kingdom of God to a pretty rough neighborhood. Hannah and Joe just take it as a given that everyone on the team will find a place to live in the area within a year or so. But some of the families are unsure if they want their kids to grow up in this kind of neighborhood, and a number of the students think that where they live now is much more central. All of these team members believe that it's not essential to live where one is doing church planting.

Put yourself in this team situation. What would you have said or thought?

M2-5-1-6 Case study 2

You are the leader of a church planting team that has met twice together to seek God, to share vision, and to begin making plans for a new church in the city. The next time you meet you ask directly how many years each team member is willing to give to this work.

Trudy and Ray answer that they're not really sure yet if they're going to be part of the team: they have to see what's going to happen before they can decide. Sarah says that she is willing to dedicate the rest of her life to this work. Wendy and Tom, who are looking for jobs, say that they're a bit reluctant to make a commitment, but if they do they'll give 100% for the next five years. Oscar, who is an incredibly talented musician, says that he's not exactly sure which university in which city he's going to be accepted to until a year and a half from now, but until then he really wants to be part of things. Peter and Suzie, who've built a house in the church-planting area, respond that as long as you're on, they're on. At the end, Kerry says that she'll be part of things as long as the team prioritizes relationships and groups above programs and fancy church services.

How would you have moved forward with a group like this?

M2-5-2 For chapter M2-2: Loved and sent – by Arne Skagen

M2-5-2-1 Team exercise 1

Tell each other on the team the experiences you've had in sharing the gospel with people, and the expectations you have in how the team can do this together in the future.

M2-5-2-2 Team exercise 2

Discuss this quote in the chapter: I've met many Christians who get a guilty conscience when others talk about doing evangelism. They know that they should share the gospel with others. But inwardly they feel that doing evangelism is a heavy burden and a distasteful duty. "If that's the way you feel about it," I always say, "then you shouldn't be sharing the gospel! Let somebody else take care of it!"

M2-5-2-3 Team exercise 3

God's love must be both our motivator and our drawing power. Do you see yourselves as a group that *others* want to be with? Are you a group of people that wants to be with others? If possible, give some concrete 'evidence' for your viewpoint.

M2-5-2-4 Individual exercises

1. How often do you pray that God will give you opportunities to share the gospel?

2. How many of your friends are unsaved?

3. How many of these unsaved friends do you regularly pray to God for their salvation?

4. When and how do you pray for them?

5. Does God ever remind you to add others to your prayer list?

6. Is God's love for you something that you often experience and rejoice over?

7. Has anyone ever remarked that they've seen God's love in and through you?

M2-5-2-5 Case study 1

A church planting team has labored almost two years and has grown to a handful of cell groups, but no one has seen anyone get saved yet. Now the team is contemplating whether or not they should begin a 'seeker-friendly' church service. They approach your group to ask your opinion on this.

What would you first ask this team before giving any advice? Each of you write some questions you would pose to the team, and share with your group your reasons for asking these particular questions.

M2-5-2-6 Case study 2

A church-planting work called New City Church has barely gotten off the ground in establishing small groups, and it's mainly been through the efforts of Oliver and Bernice that new people are even invited to the church. Oliver and Bernice seem to have a natural ability to get to know people, to invite them to a meeting and to share Jesus with them. The rest of the church has enough to do in just keeping up with the new people Oliver and Bernice bring along. But these two have suddenly found out that they'll be moving to Australia, Bernice having earlier applied at her business to be part of a new branch office opening there. Around this time the church-planting leader suggests that the core leadership team should take a 'spiritual gifts' test, which reveals that none of them have 'evangelism' as one of their three-top spiritual gifts (the leader has it in fourth-place, after 'mercy', 'teaching' and 'leadership'). This makes the team a bit disgruntled.

How would you encourage them? How would you advise them?

M2-5-3 For chapter M2-3: The harvest is ripe – by Arne Skagen

M2-5-3-1 Team exercise 1

Let everyone on the team map-out his or her own relational networks. The first time around, include everyone that anyone talks with at least once a week. Then compare each other's networks. Share with each other about them. Discover any relational overlaps between the various networks. Count how many individuals the team actually comes in contact with in a given week.

M2-5-3-2 Team exercise 2

Look at the team's networks one more time, then ask the Holy Spirit to show you who among these relationships is ripe for the harvest: Who do you experience as being positive to you? Who listens to you when you share your faith? Who asks provocative questions? Who is it that knocks on your door when they need practical help, who comes to you with their personal problems? In other words – or in the words of Jesus in Luke 10 – who are the people of peace in your network?

M2-5-3-3 Team exercise 3

Share with your team members your personal testimony in how you gave your life to Jesus. Or tell them how you believe the gospel can be shared with others in a simple, succinct yet understandable way.

M2-5-3-4 Individual exercises

Write your personal testimony in less than 200 words, and include the following elements: 1) Before I gave my life to Jesus, 2) How I gave my life to Jesus, and 3) How life is together with Jesus.

Make your own prayer list for people in your network who you feel the Holy Spirit is speaking to you about.

Ask the Holy Spirit to help you write a short presentation of the gospel (no more than 200 words) custom-made for each person on your prayer list.

M2-5-3-5 Case study 1

Jake and Terry work together at the office. One day, out of the blue, Jake asks Terry, "Terry, are you a Christian?" Terry never once dared to bring up the topic of faith on the job, so he was a bit put-out but answered nonetheless. "Yeah, uh, why do you ask?" Now Jake was the one who was a bit put-out, "Well, I'm not sure exactly – the thought just dropped into my head yesterday, that maybe you were a Christian. I can't quite explain it....". "Are *you* a Christian, then?" asks Terry back. "Me?! No way," said Jake. "But do you believe that God exists?" asks Terry back. Sure, Jake was pretty sure of this. And he had tried to read the Bible lately, but he felt it was just a bit difficult to understand. He tried to read a book in the Bible by this guy named Joel...

How would you continue this conversation? Is Jake 'ripe for the harvest'?

M2-5-3-6 Case study 2

Wendy complains about never having led anyone to Jesus. She easily connects with new people to have deep and meaningful conversations. She also speaks quite freely about her faith and what it means to her. But when it comes to challenging people to make a decision, she feels like a total coward. She finds the whole thing scary.

» Do you challenge Wendy to go against her personality – and her fear?

» What could help Wendy to become more free?

» How would you advise Wendy in she could do when speaking to her new friends about God?

M2-5-4 For chapter M2-4: "I have fully preached the gospel" – by Arnt Jakob Holvik

M2-5-4-1 Team exercise 1

Who, where and in what way does the team reach out on a regular basis to non-Christians with the gospel of Jesus Christ and the power of God?

M2-5-4-2 Team exercise 2

What specific actions can you as a team put to life to reach more non-Christians with the good news? Focus on strategic initiatives that can be maintained over time.

M2-5-4-3 Individual exercises

» On a scale of 1 to 10, how comfortable do you feel in asking to pray for people's needs? 1 is not comfortable at all and 10 is very comfortable.

» How comfortable to you feel (on the same scale) in asking: "Has anyone ever explained to you how to become a Christian? Would you like for me to explain it to you—it'll only take a few minutes?"

» What would it take to for you to increase your boldness in sharing the gospel?

M2-5-4-4 Case study 1

It's been almost a year since your team started working on planting a new church. Your team consists of five dedicated people, and has come in contact with five other local Christians who'd like to support you in the church-planting ministry. You feel really excited about this.

On the other hand, the team has not yet led any non-believers to Christ. They've made some attempts at building relationships with non-believers, but without much success.

The team and the local believers pray that people will get saved, and some have a real expectation that this will happen. They ask for your opinion; you see that they've actually had very little contact with non-Christians, and that there seems to be a lot of fear in the group about sharing the gospel of Jesus Christ with the ones they meet.

» The team turns to you for some advice, so what would you say?

» How would you advise them?

M2-5-4-5 Case study 2

One day Andrew on the church planting team meets a member of the church council from a traditional church in the area.

The team has had quite close contact with the workers at the traditional church, but Andrew is now confronted with the uncomfortable fact that some people from the church are upset because they saw people from the team pray for a couple of teenaged boys on the street, laying hands on them while they prayed.

One of the boys they prayed for had a problem with diabetes, and the other one had crutches to support his broken foot. Paul knows that what they did was fully consistent with the Bible—both Jesus and the apostles did this—and the boy on crutches actually got his foot healed, or at least that's what he said as he walked away carrying his crutches on his shoulder. The other boy with diabetes was asked to check out his condition with his doctor.

Andrew was told that the church council in the traditional church had received this as a subject of issue after three people filed a complaint in the church. The ones who complained argue that this kind of prayer can lead to "abuse" and "trespassing on other people's privacy" for those who are not familiar with this kind of practice—it should stay in the "private sphere." Paul also finds out that they are considering going to the local newspapers.

How would you deal with a situation like this?

M2-5-5 Learning goals and checklist for church planting

In the following section you will find the learning goals we've made for the main themes in the book. We would like you now to evaluate yourself and what you've learned. Some of the learning goals are meant to help you to reflect on the understanding and acquisition of knowledge you've received, as well as reflect on the actual church-planting process you and your team has gone through. Other tasks are more concrete, and we believe that they are important for your team to work through. Below you will find the numbers 1 to 5 in relation to the learning goals: 1 means "I have not worked seriously with this goal or looked at the tasks related to it" while 5 means "I have acquired a good understanding, reflected on, and worked through the tasks related to the learning goal." 2-4 is somewhere in between. We hope it goes well with your evaluation.

M2-5-5-1 [M2-1 Pioneer work and comfort zones – by Øystein Gjerme]

○ ○ ○ ○ ○
1 2 3 4 5

I have an understanding of church planting as pioneer work and the challenges a church planter might face in his or her daily life.

○ ○ ○ ○ ○
1 2 3 4 5

I understand the importance of clarifying who our team's target group is, as well as the importance of understanding the culture we are planting in.

○ ○ ○ ○ ○
1 2 3 4 5

I recognize some of the comfort zones in my own life, and understand that a church-planting ministry may require that I break some of them in order to reach the goals of the church planting team.

M2-5-5-2 [M2-2 Loved and sent – by Arne Skagen]

○ ○ ○ ○ ○
1 2 3 4 5

I understand that the basis of evangelism is the love of God within us, together with our obedience in response to the Holy Spirit.

○ ○ ○ ○ ○
1 2 3 4 5

I understand how the Christian community in itself is evangelical and how we are interdependent on each other to communicate the gospel.

M2-5-5-3 [M2-3 The harvest is ripe – by Arne Skagen]

○ ○ ○ ○ ○
1 2 3 4 5

I have gained an understanding in how to recognize when the harvest is ripe, and how God works with people in the various phases of the journey toward faith.

○ ○ ○ ○ ○
1 2 3 4 5

I know how to map-out each team member's social network and have learned ways a team can reach new people.

○ ○ ○ ○ ○
1 2 3 4 5

I have become more knowledgeable in how to share the gospel with others.

M2-5-5-4 [M2-4 I have fully preached the gospel – by Arnt Jakob Holvik]

○ ○ ○ ○ ○
1 2 3 4 5

I am aware of the power that lies within the gospel's testimony of Jesus.

○ ○ ○ ○ ○
1 2 3 4 5

I understand the need for the Holy Spirit's power and confirmation of preaching through healing, signs and wonders.

○ ○ ○ ○ ○
1 2 3 4 5

I am able to design a practical plan for how the team can work together in outreach.

Recommended literature list for M1 and M2

Here you will find a list of books we've enjoyed and have used in our work in church planting. It includes titles that address leadership, strategy and different models for church planting and evangelism. Most of the English books are available on amazon.com or amazon.co.uk. The easiest way of finding the Norwegian books is doing a Google search, if you can't find them at bokkilden.no. Our hope with this list is that it might provide you with relevant literature for the challenges you face.

Addison, Steve. *How to Know if You Should Plant a Church*. Baronia, Victoria, Australia: Church Resource Ministries Australia, 1993.

Appelton, Joanne. ECPN Concept Paper: Mid Sized Mission - The Use of Mid Sized Groups as a Vital Strategic Component of Church Planting. Published on Leadnet.org, 2008.

Bakke, Ray. *A Theology as Big as the City*. Downers Grove, IL: Inter Varsity Press, 1997.

Barker, Joel Arthur. *Paradigms: The Business of Discovering the Future*. New York: Harper Business, 1994.

Beckham, William A. *The Second Reformation*. Houston, TX: TOUCH publications, 1997.

Bosch, David. Transforming Mission: Paradigm Shifts in Theology of Mission. Maryknoll: Orbis, 1991.

Breen, Mike and Hopkins, Bob. Clusters: Creative Mid-Sized Missional. Sheffield: ACPI, 2008.

Cordeiro, Wayne. *Doing Church as a Team*. Ventura, CA: Gospel Light Publications, 2001.

Cladis, Georg. *Leading the Team-Based Church*. West Sussex: Jossey-Bass, 1999.

Cole, Neil. *Organic Church*. San Francisco: Jossey-Bass, 2005.

Comiskey, Joel T. Planting Churches that Reproduce: Starting a Network of Simple Churches. Lima, OH: CCS Publishing, 2009.

Comiskey, Joel T. Home Cell Group Explosion: How Your Small Group Can Grow and Multiply. Houston, TX: TOUCH Publications, 2002.

Comiskey, Joel T. *Leadership Explosion*. Houston, TX: TOUCH Publications, 2008.

Donders, Paul Christian. *Creative Life Planning: Discover Your Calling, Develop Your Potential*. Kristiansand, Norway. Sidevedside forlag, 2008.

Donders, Paul Christian and Jaap, Ketelaar. *Value Centered Leadership in Church and Organizations*. Argyll: Xpand, 2011.

Ferguson, Dave and Ferguson, Jon. Exponential: How You and Your Friends Can Start a Missional Church Movement (Exponential Series). Grand Rapids: Zondervan, 2010.

Frost, Michael and Hirsh, Alan. *The shaping of things to come,* Peabody, MA: Hendrickson, 2003.

Frost, Michael. *Exiles: Living Missionally in a Post-Christian Culture*. Peabody, MA: Hendrickson Publisher, 2006.

Gibbs, Eddie. *Leadership Next*. Downers Grove, IL: Intervarsity, 2005.

Greg, Pete and Blackwell, David. *24-7 Prayer Manual*. Colorado Springs: David C. Cook, 2010

Guder, Darrell L. and Barrett, Lois. Missional Church - A Vision for the Sending of the Church in North America. Grand Rapids: Eerdmans, 1998.

Halter, Hugh and Smay, Matt. *DNA: The Gathered and Scattered Church*. Grand Rapids: Zondervan, 2010.

Hirsch, Allan. *The Forgotten Ways*. Grand Rapids: Brazos press, 2006.

Hirsch, Allan and Frost, Michael. *ReJesus: A Wild Messiah for a Missional Church*. Edinburgh: Hendrickson Publisher, 2009.

Hirsh, Allan and Frost, Michael. *The Shaping of the Things to Come*. Edinburgh: Hendrickson Publisher, 2001.

Hybles, Bill. *Becoming a Contagious Christian*. Grand Rapids: Zondervan, 1996.

Hopkins, Bob and Mary. *Church Planting Coaching Manual*. Sheffield: Anglican Church Planting Initiative, 2003.

Hunter III, George G. *The Celtic Way of Evangelism:* Nashville: Abingdon, 2000.

Jacobsen, Leif S. The Leadership Factor in Church Planting Projects in Norway from 1990 to 2000. Virginia Beach: Regent University, 2005.

Kotter, John P. *A Sense of Urgency*. Boston: Harvard Business, 2008.

Kotter, John P. *Leading Change*. Boston, Harvard Business School Press, 1996

Kreider, Larry. *House Church Networks: A Church for a New Generation*. Lititz, PA: House to House Publications, 2001.

Malm, Magnus. I lammets tegn - om den kristne kirkes vei inn i et nytt årtusen. Oslo: Luther, 1996.

Malm, Magnus. *Vägvisere, en bok om kristent lederskap*. Uppsala: EFS forlag, 1990.

Malphurs, Aubrey. *Values-Driven Leadership*. Grand Rapids: Baker Books, 1996.

Malphurs, Aubrey. Advanced Strategic Planning: A New Model for Church and Ministry Leaders. Grand Rapids: Baker Books, 1999.

Malphurs, Aubrey. Planting Growing Churches for the 21st Century: A Comprehensive Guide for New Churches and Those Desiring Renewal, 2nd ed. Grand Rapids: Baker Books, 1998.

Maxwell, John. *The 17 Indisputable Laws of Teamwork*. Nashville: Thomas Nelson, 2001.

McClung, Floyd and Kreider, Larry. *The Cry for Spiritual Fathers and Mothers*. Lititz, PA: House to House Publications, 2002.

McLaren, Brian. More Ready Than You Realize: The Power of Everyday Conversations. Grand Rapids: Zondervan, 2002.

McNeal, Reggie. Revolution in Leadership: Training Apostles for Tomorrow's Church. Nashville, TN: Abingdon Press, 1999.

Murray, Stuart and Wilkinson-Heys, Anne. *Hope from the Margins - New Ways of Being Church*. Cambridge, UK: Grove Books, 2000.

Neighbour, Ralph W. Where do we go from Here? A Guidebook for the Cell Group Church. Houston, TX: TOUCH Publications, 2000.

Ott, Craig and Wilson, Gene. *Global Church Planting: Biblical Principles and Best Practices for Multiplication*. Grand Rapids: Baker Academic, 2011.

Patrick, Darren. *Church Planter: The Man, the Message, the Mission. Wheaton: Crossway, 2010.*

Paul D. Stanley and Clinton, J. Robert. *Connecting: The Mentoring Relationships You Need to Succeed in Life*. Colorado Springs: NavPress, 1992.

Pippert, Rebecca M. Out of the Saltshaker and into the World, Evangelism as a Way of Life (new edition). Downers Grove, IL. Inter Varsity Press, 2010.

Reinhart, Stacy T. *Upside Down – the paradox in servant leadership*. Colorado Springs: NavPress, 1998

Robinson, Martin and Smith, Dwight. *Invading Secular Space*. Oxford: Monarch, 2003.

Robinson, Martin. *Planting Mission-Shaped Churches Today*. Oxford: Monarch, 2006.

Rolfsen, Ommund and Dahle, Terje. *Utrustende lederskap*. Evenskjær: K-Vekst, 2004.

Roxburgh Allan J, and Romanuk, Fred. *The Missional Leader, Equipping your Church to Reach a Changing world*. San Francisco: Jossey-Bass, 2006.

Schwartz, Christian and Logan, Robert E. *Natural Church Development: A Guide to Eight Essential Qualities of Healthy Churches*. Saint Charles, IL: Churchsmart Resources, 1996.

Simson, Wolfgang. *Houses that Change the World*. Authentic, 2001.

Skagen, Arne. Endelig mandag. Hverdagsevangelisering for alle. Ottestad: Prokla Media, 2012.

Ski, Martin. Fram til Urkristendommen, Pinsevekkelsen Gjennom 50 år. Oslo: Filadelfiaforlaget, 1957.

Sørensen, Sten and Rolfsen, Ommund. *Menighetsplanting på norsk*. Oslo: Rex, 1996.

Stanley, Andy. *The next Generation Leader*. Portland, OR: Multnomah Press, 2006.

Stetzer, Ed. *Planting Missional Churches*. Nashville, TN: Broadman & Holman Publishers, 2006.

Strauch, Alexander. *Biblical Eldership*. Colorado Springs: Lewis & Roth Publishers, 1997.

Surratt, Geoff, Ligon, Greg and Bird, Varren. *The Multi-Site Church Revolution*. Grand Rapids: Zondervan, 2011.

Tangen, Karl Inge. Ecclesial Identification Beyond Transactional Individualism? A Case Study of Life Strategies in Growing Late Modern Churches. PhD thesis, Oslo; MF Norwegian School of Theology, 2009.

Thumma, Scott and Travis, Dave. *Beyond Megachurch Myths*. San Francisco: Jossey-Bass, 2007.

Timmis, Steve and Chester, Tim. *Total Church, a Radical Reshaping around Gospel and Community*. Wheaton, IL: Crossway books, 2008.

Wagner, C. Peter and Comiskey, Joel T. *Cell Group Explosion: How Your Small Group Can Grow and Multiply*. Houston, TX: TOUCH Publication, 2002.

Warren, Robert. Being Human, Being Church – Spirituality and Mission in the Local Church. London: Marshall Pickering, 1995.

Wheatley, Margaret J. *Leadership and the New Science*. San Francisco: Berrett-Koehler, 2001.

Whitmore, John. *Coaching for Performance*. San Diego: Pfeiffer, 2002.

Williams, Rowan et. al. Mission-shaped church; church planting and fresh expressions of church in a changing context. London: Church House Publishing, 2004.

Wilson, Scott. Challenge of Leadership, What Leaders do Next. Denmark: Royal, 2007.

Printed in Germany
by Amazon Distribution
GmbH, Leipzig